# landscape
# design today

Author: Arian Mostaedi

Publishers: Carles Broto & Josep Maria Minguet

Editorial Coordination: Jacobo Krauel

Architectural Adviser: Pilar Chueca

Graphic Design & Production: Héctor Navarro

Text: Contributed by the architects,
edited by Amber Ockrassa and Jacobo Krauel

Cover photo: © Jeroen Musch / West 8

© Carles Broto (All languages, except Spanish)
Ausias Marc 20, 4-2. 08010 Barcelona, Spain
Tel.: +34 933 012 199  Fax: +34 933 026 797
www.linksbooks.net · info@linksbooks.net

ISBN: 84-89861-97-8
D.L.: 41.476
Printed in Barcelona, Spain

# landscape
## design today

# index

8      **Introduction**

10     Gigon / Guyer architects **Museum und Park Kalkriese**

22     Jensen & Skodvin **Mountain Road Project**

32     Michèle & Miquel **Parque Natural "Les Bouillouses"**

42     Topotek 1 **Postindustrial Park**

52     Claudi Aguiló **Parc Els Pinetons**

58     Agence Ter .de **Landesgartenschau "Aqua Magica 2000"**

66     West 8 **Expo 02-Swiss National Expo**

80     West 8 **Sund Garden**

86     Claudio Vekstein **Paseo de la Costa del Río de la Plata**

100    Miguel Centellas, Olga Tarrasó, Julià Espinàs & Teresa Galí **Parque de la Alpujarra**

106    Shuhei Endo **Springtecture H**

112    Gruppe F **The Meadow Park on the Wuhle**

120    Latz + Partner **Landscape Park Duisburg Nord**

124    Imma Jansana Ferrer **Jardines de Àngel Guimerà**

132    Jõao Álvaro Rocha **Parque de Lazer de Moutidos**

142    Kovács, Lendvai, Muszbek, Pozsár, Tihanyi & Wallner **Millenáris Park**

150    Stig L. Andersson **The Anchor Park**

158    Florence Mercier **Le Grand Mail du Parc des Lilas**

168    Ramón Pico + Javier López **Sendero del Pinar de la Algaida**

# introduction

Although Landscape Design as a formal branch of study has only existed since relatively recent times, the concept of reshaping our natural surroundings is as old as humankind's written history.

In the 3rd century BCE, the Greeks were putting Euclidean geometry into practice in their ideas behind how landscape should be sculpted. Pliny the Younger gives us an early landscaping reference in a letter written in the 1st century in which he speaks of the practicality of using boxwood hedges for partitioning the landscape in his estate gardens. The marvels of Kublai Khan's gardens at Xanadu ("fully sixteen miles of parkland well watered with springs and streams and diversified with lawns") were recorded by Marco Polo several centuries later. The classical French garden, with its formal lines and tidily trimmed shrubbery, arose during the reign of Louis XIV; while the English writer Alexander Pope would later help usher in the ascendancy of informal landscape design with his ideas: "in all, let nature never be forgot... Consult the genius of the place".

In all, a dizzying proliferation of styles have characterized how the human race has chosen to impose its will on its natural surroundings over the centuries. And as with any other school of design, landscaping is in large part a reflection of our cultural values.

So when we started analyzing the sort of projects that would be representative of a book entitled Landscape Design Today - the sort of projects that would somehow reflect the culture in which we live - we quickly realized that landscape design today is as heterogeneous as the world around us and that, like our culture, no one trend predominates.

Rather, what we find are amalgamations, pieces taken from the "best of" a given era or locale, an overlapping of formal and informal elements - all displaying the unique thumbprint of the designer or of the place itself and all stubbornly defying definition.

If any one concept could be said to encapsulate the current state of landscape design, it would have to be "diversity".

With that, enjoy this diverse and delightful collection of some of the finest examples of Landscape Design Today!

# Gigon / Guyer architects + Zulauf Seippel Schweingruber, landscape architects
## Museum und Park Kalkriese
Kalkriese, Germany

The site for this commission is an agricultural parcel (approx. 20 Ha) that is considered to be the long-sought location of the famous battle of the Teutons against the Romans in the year 9 C.E.: the Battle of Varus.

The probable course of the Roman legion's route along the rampart has been retraced by means of large, irregularly placed iron plates laid out along the ground, comprising a footpath. These plates are engraved with historical, Roman and contemporary written fragments. Proceeding from iron plate to iron plate and collecting fragments of information (like archeologists) from the ground, an image of the historical battle situation develops step by step within the visitor's minds.

By contrast, narrow paths strewn with wood chips form a net-like pattern that represents the Teuton's positions in the forest.

The location and assumed height of the former Teutonic earthen rampart, including palisades built on top, have been marked by means of iron poles. Where archeological proof of the rampart's existence is at hand, the iron bars have been placed more closely together. Where they have been placed farther apart, the location of the earlier ramparts is open to speculation.

Landscape design measures aimed at visualizing the original site (course of the terrain, make-up of the ground) were simply realized

with the means of contemporary agrarian cultivation. The existing forest has been supplemented with trees to the south in order to trace its former edge. To the north, it was partially cleared to form fields in order to render the expanse of the former moor landscape.

Three pavilions (centered on the themes of seeing, hearing and questioning) on the field both broaden and put into perspective the impressions gained outdoors.

The museum consists of a one-story volume and a tower-like structure. The actual exhibition is to be found in the torso of the building, where a darkened, undivided room allows for the unfettered staging of the manifold themes of this battle.

As a functional supplement to the museum and park, an existing farm has been converted into a visitor's center, where there are a restaurant, children's museum, conference rooms, and offices for both the administration and the archeologists. The latter will continue to excavate and conduct research into the battle ground in the coming years, contributing new finds and insights, and thus continuing to write the history of the battle.

**Photographs: Heinrich Helfenstein**

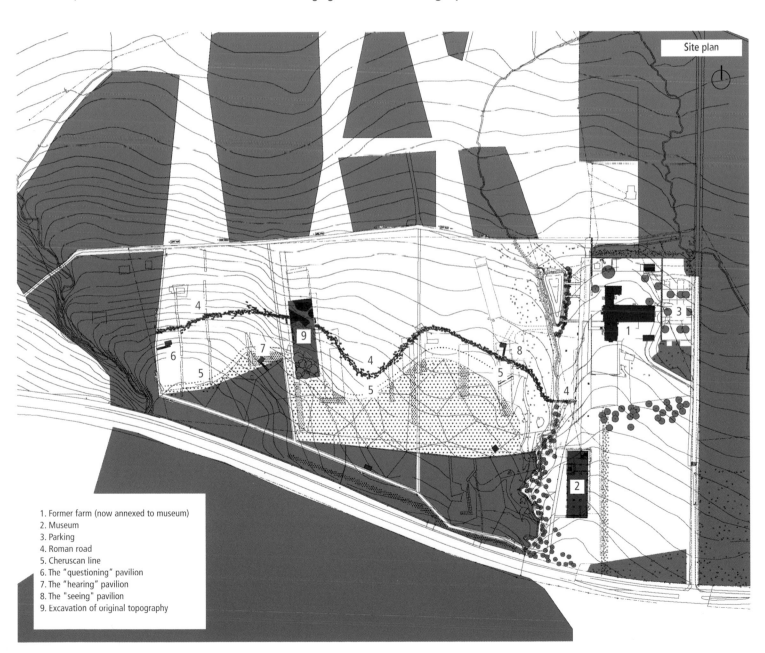

Site plan

1. Former farm (now annexed to museum)
2. Museum
3. Parking
4. Roman road
5. Cheruscan line
6. The "questioning" pavilion
7. The "hearing" pavilion
8. The "seeing" pavilion
9. Excavation of original topography

The probable course of the Roman legion's route along the rampart has been retraced by means of large irregularly placed iron plates, each of which is inscribed with historical or contemporary information, thus guiding visitors through the battle site. Other path networks are delineated by wood chips and gravel.

The "hearing" pavilion is equipped with a large pipe that transmits the amplified sounds of the outside world into a soundproofed room. Inside, a pipe can be turned by hand and directed toward exterior sources of sounds.

**The "hearing" pavilion**

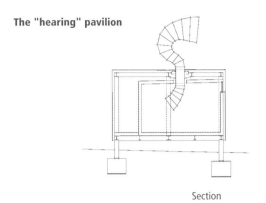

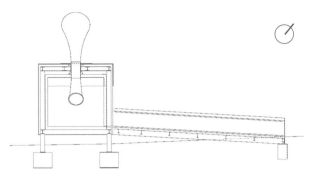

Section

Longitudinal section

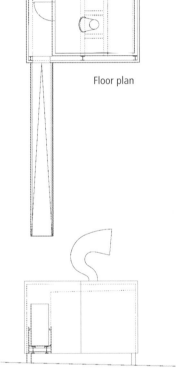

Floor plan

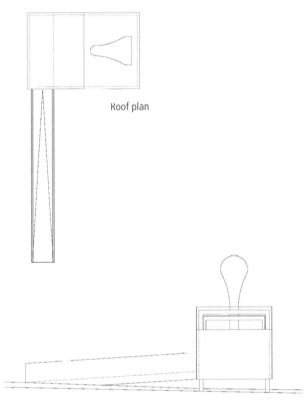

Roof plan

South-East Elevation

South-West Elevation

13

**The "seeing" pavilion**

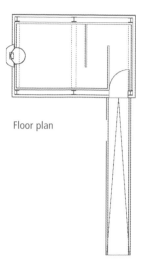

Floor plan

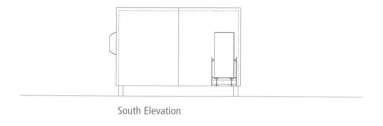

South Elevation

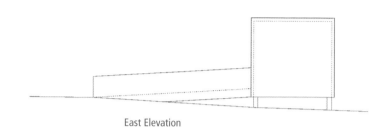

East Elevation

0        4m

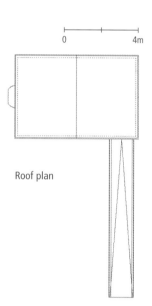

Roof plan

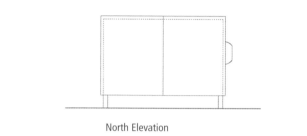

North Elevation

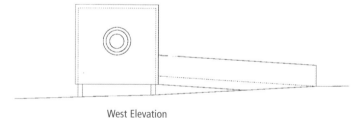

West Elevation

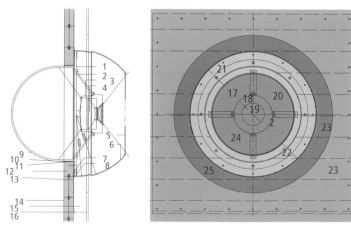

Construction detail of the "seeing" pavilion's eye

# The "questioning" pavilion

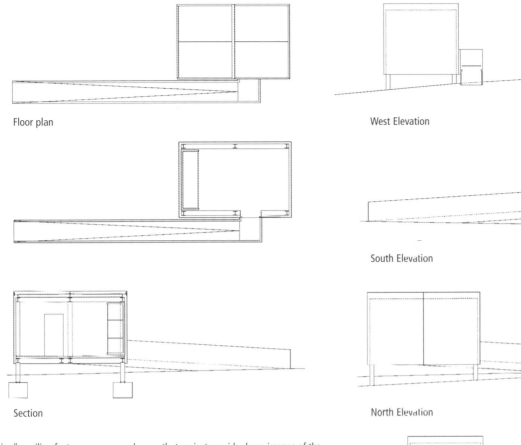

Floor plan

West Elevation

Section

South Elevation

North Elevation

East Elevation

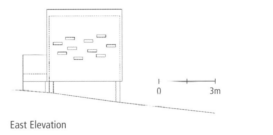

The "seeing" pavilion features a camera obscura that projects upside-down images of the exterior world onto a glowing half-sphere. Akin to the function of the human eyeball, what one sees is projected upon this over-sized, glass "retina". Without electricity, this glass half-sphere casts a mystical glow into the darkened room.

Inside the "questioning" pavilion, a wall with slit-like openings faces a wall with nine television monitors, where a compilation of current news broadcasts show how, to this day, conflicts continue to be fought with aggression and violence.

1. Support ring external radius = 530mm, internal radius = 340 mm
2. Crosspieces, 4 pieces
3. Lens frame
4. Objective with four lenses
5. Glass with solar protection, used according to assembly, detachable
6. Roof, protection from climatic conditions, 6 mm hot galvanized steel, external radius = 540mm
7. 5-8mm compression band
8. Long-lasting elasticized hermetic sealant
9. Sandblasted plexiglass, d=12mm, external radius = 400mm
10. Long-lasting elasticized hermetic sealant
11. 5-8mm compression band
12. Wood massing elements: d=80mm
13. Plate, d=1.5mm black matte cladding, with drip-proof edge, affixed to wooden struc-

ture, sealed with silicone, in situ dap d=810mm after assembly of steel face (as with wood construction)
14. Black matte layer
15. Ventilation system, d=110mm
16. Sandblasted sheets of steel, 15mm
17. Glass with solar protection
18. Lens frame
19. Optics system
20. Crosspieces
21. Support ring
22. Roof, protection from climatic conditions
23. Wood support
24. Plexiglass
25. Plate, d=1.5mm black matte cladding, with drip-proof edge, affixed to wooden structure, sealed with silicone, in situ dap d=810mm after assembly of steel face (as with wood construction)

Museum. Floor plan -1                Floor plan 0                Floor plan +1

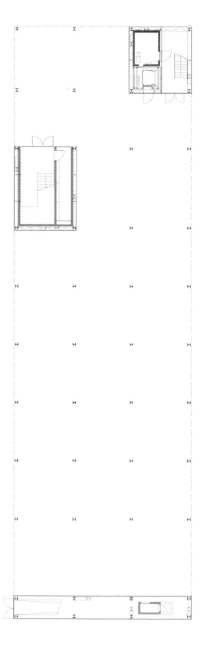
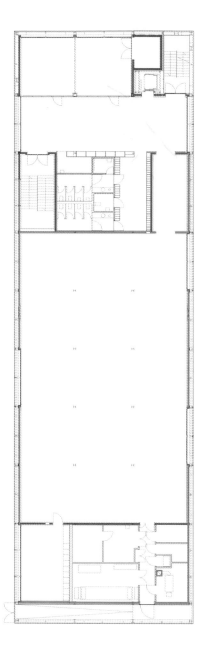
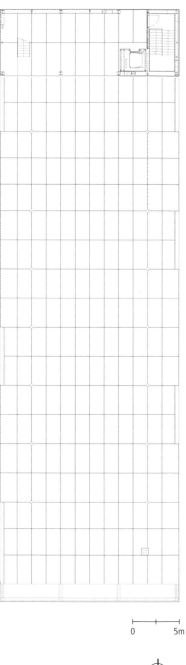

0       5m

The museum consists of a one-story volume and a tower-like structure. The landscape and the one-time battlefield can be taken in with a bird's eye view from nearly 40 meters above the ground. Like the pavilions, the museum is constructed with a steel skeleton and clad with large, rusting steel plates. Steel plates have also been used within the heated interior part of the museum as cladding (rolled steel plates for the wall and ceiling and non-rusting steel for the floor plates).

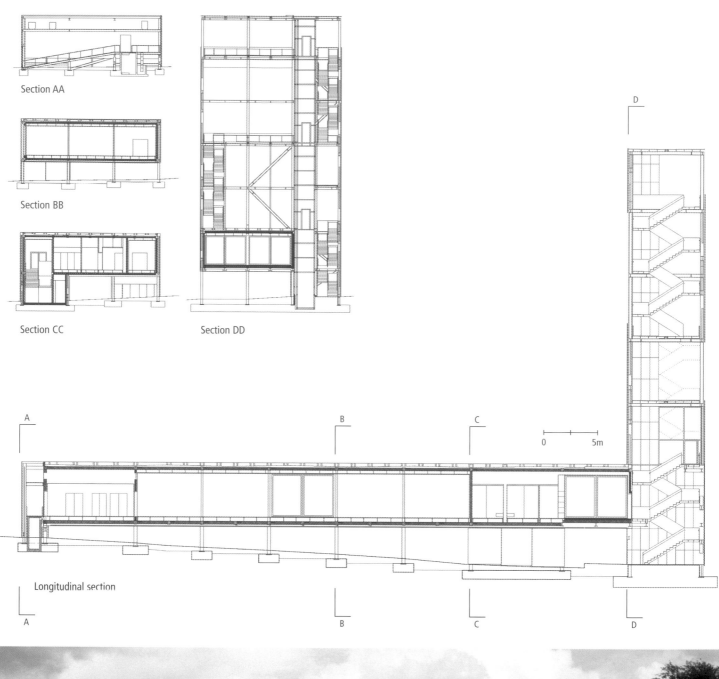

Section AA

Section BB

Section CC

Section DD

D

A

B

C

D

0   5m

Longitudinal section

A

B

C

D

North elevation

South elevation

East elevation

0    5m

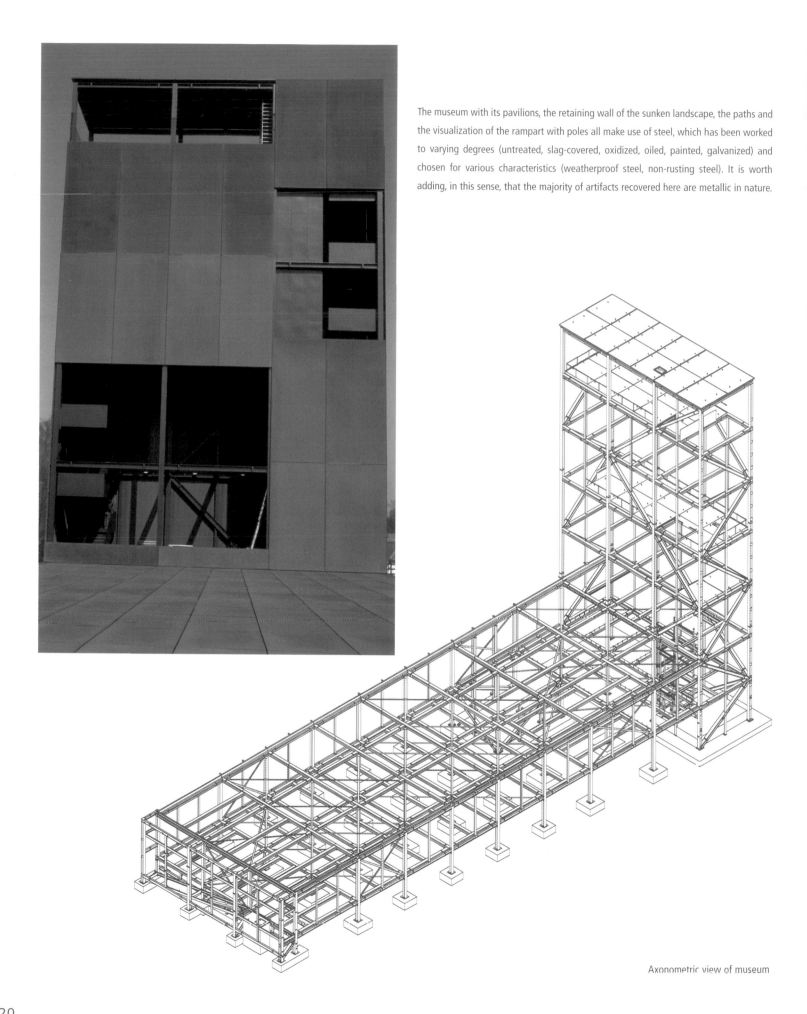

The museum with its pavilions, the retaining wall of the sunken landscape, the paths and the visualization of the rampart with poles all make use of steel, which has been worked to varying degrees (untreated, slag-covered, oxidized, oiled, painted, galvanized) and chosen for various characteristics (weatherproof steel, non-rusting steel). It is worth adding, in this sense, that the majority of artifacts recovered here are metallic in nature.

Axonometric view of museum

# Jensen & Skodvin
## Mountain Road Project ]
Sognefjellet, Norway

A Tourism Project has been undertaken in recent years under the auspices of the Norwegian Department of Transportation in a number of districts. The intent of the project is to rectify the relative absence of offerings for travelers along the most popular tourist routes. The project area lies along Sognefjellsvegen from Lom to Gaupne, and along Strynefjellsvegen from Grotli to Oppstryn. These roads provide an especially attractive route for tourists, running through spectacular Norwegian mountain landscapes, and as roads they represent interesting architectonic qualities in and of themselves.

The planned projects, some of which have reached completion, treat a broad spectrum of programs, from the development of new roadside elements (signage, railing, information systems, furniture) to the establishment of rest areas and stopping points.

The projects have been founded and developed at two distinct topological levels. One is that of localized interventions (or stopping points), which each site geometrically determines, and which thus cannot be repeated (rest area floors, for example). This kind of project allows for large geometric leeway, and can be formed freely without affecting functionality. The other level deals with general objects that can be produced serially and employed in various places. These objects relate geometry to function, thus reducing the degree of freedom to deviate (furnishing, railings, restrooms, and so forth). These objects are not dependent on locality, and can be placed freely. Taken as a whole, they represent a "catalogue" of elements that can be employed to meet any requirement.

The projects in general are an attempt to clarify the surrounding landscape in a number of ways, primarily by supplementing elements that reveal the geometry of nature.

**Photographs: Jan Olar Jenser**

Site plan

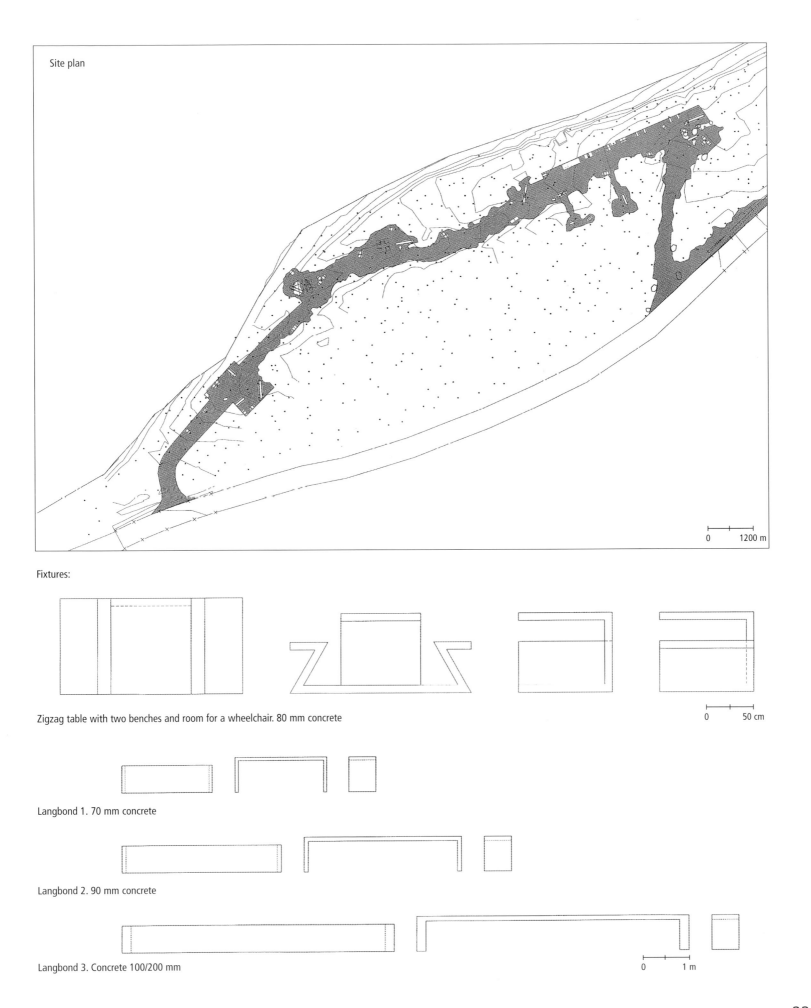

0   1200 m

Fixtures:

Zigzag table with two benches and room for a wheelchair. 80 mm concrete

0   50 cm

Langbond 1. 70 mm concrete

Langbond 2. 90 mm concrete

Langbond 3. Concrete 100/200 mm

0   1 m

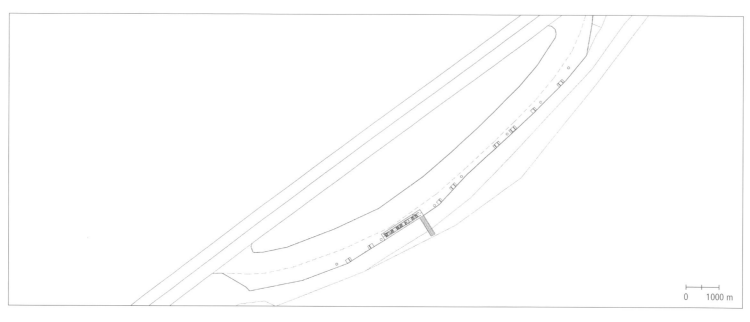

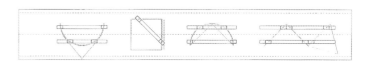

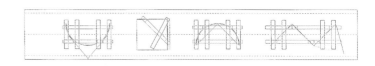

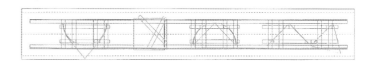

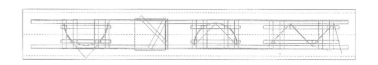

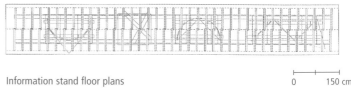

Information stand floor plans

0        150 cm

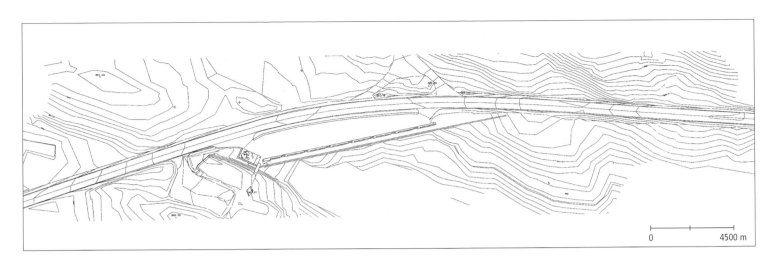

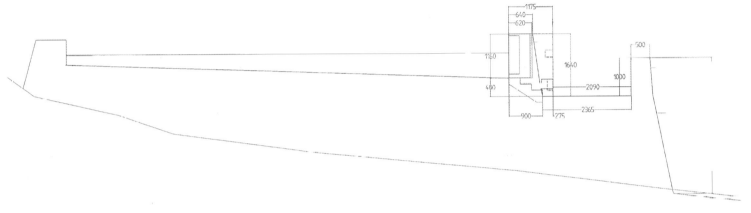

0          4500 m

The Gaupne information point consists of pine logs stacked to a height of 2.4 meters, and running a length of 37 meters. Prefabricated concrete elements comprise the roof. The intention was to create a monotony of materiality that would provide an unobtrusive backdrop for the information and display cases.

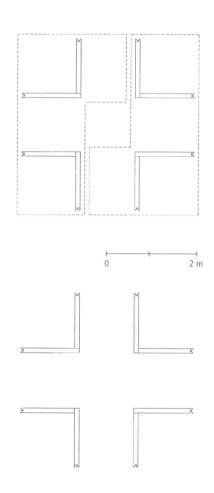

The Liasanden rest area is formed in a slight declivity that runs like a riverbed and that has been filled with gravel to the necessary level. As such, the need for any blasting and digging has been eliminated. The level of the gravel need not be uniform, so that the upper surface rises and falls according to the situation. The tree trunks have been protected from possible damage with wooden splints and hemp rope.

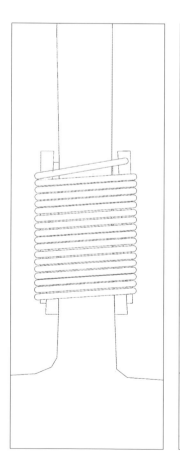

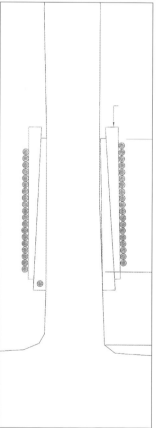

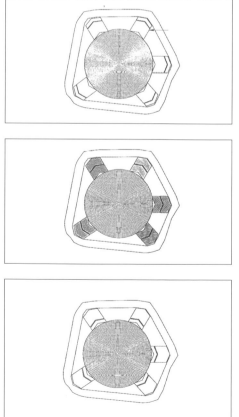

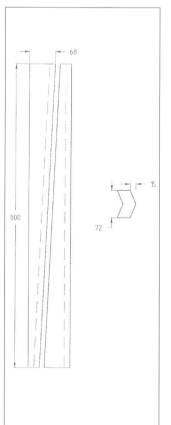

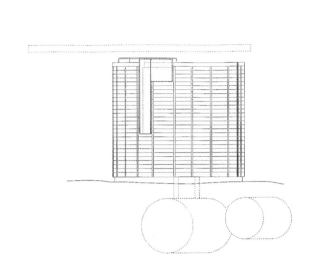

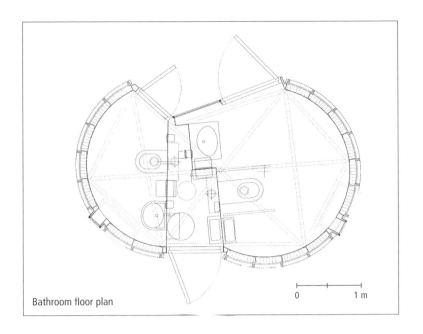

Bathroom floor plan

0        1 m

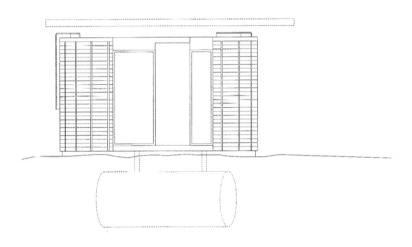

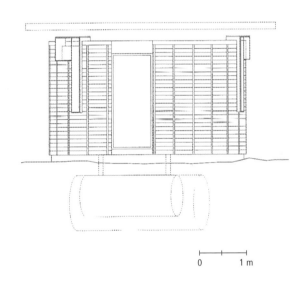

Bathroom elevations

0        1 m

The rock where the scenic lookout at Videseter Falls is located had been blasted long ago to allow for greater accessibility. The railing is of 90 mm steel rod, which is cast in holes drilled at the same datum at the edge as elsewhere at the lookout. In concert with steel plates, this technique resulted in a highly stable geometry, which functions like a horizontal truss. The steel has been bent in situ, as its curves were impossible to represent on paper. The zigzag formation of the railing significantly reduces the danger of collapse due to heavy snowfall.

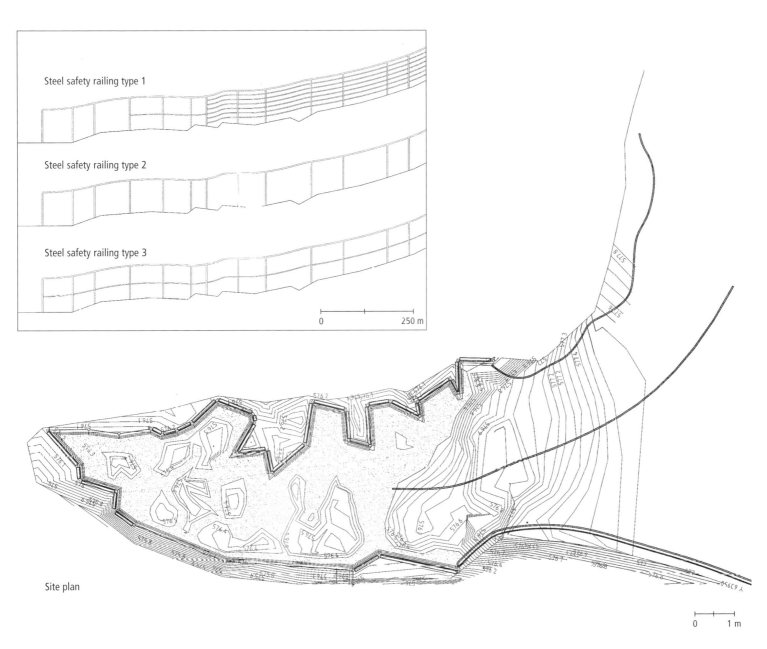

Steel safety railing type 1

Steel safety railing type 2

Steel safety railing type 3

0       250 m

Site plan

0     1 m

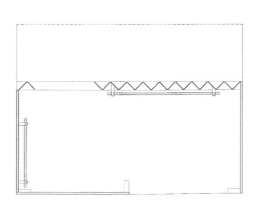

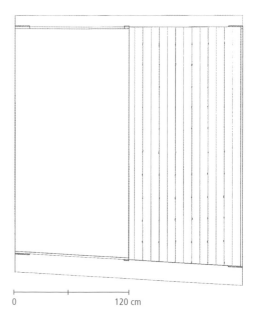

0       120 cm

Site plan

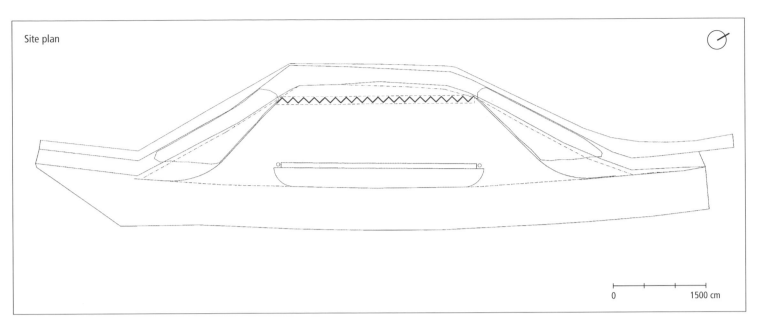

0          1500 cm

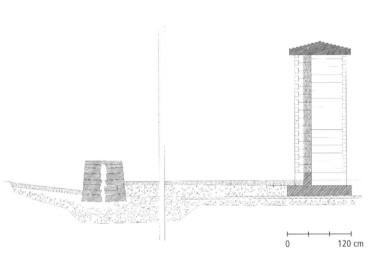

0          120 cm

A simple structure of oxidized Core-10 steel with concrete flooring and a prefabricated concrete slab roof comprise a shelter for cyclists along the road.
An information point and picnic area with simple concrete tables and wooden and steel benches have been placed at the end of a peninsula in Vagamo Lake.

### Michèle & Miquel
### Michèle Orliac Runuy, Miquel Batlle Pagès
## Parque Natural "Les Bouillouses"
Pla de Barrès, France

Near the city of Mont-Lluis, at the northern tip of the French Cerdanya, rises the massif Carlit: a peak of 2921 meters in height. At the foot of the massif is a large hydroelectric reservoir called Les Bulloses, which was constructed at the start of the 20th century. The influx of visitors to Les Bulloses during the summer months had reached such worrying levels (because of an increase in visual and environmental contamination, due especially to heavy vehicle traffic), that the French government decided to restrict vehicle access in the summer and to create a large parking area at the entrance. This is the first phase of a public transport service to and from the reservoir.

The area known as Pla de Barrès was chosen for the project's installations, which include a 600-vehicle parking lot covering 9000 m², bus stops, information pavilions and footpaths linking the various components of the complex.

The parking lot is divided into four large rectangular platforms arranged along displaced axes, somewhat like train compartments. Each platform follows the slope of the natural terrain. In order to minimize the impact that such a large asphalted surface full of cars might have, the surrounding vegetation was included in the design scheme.

The path of vegetation traces a zig-zagging route through and around the parking platforms, which in turn lead into the forest, toward the bus stops. A concrete slab (poured in situ) finished with a border of corten steel was chosen for the walkway. Its continuity confers unity onto the different legs of the route, underlines the ruptures in the relief design and highlights the opposition of a concrete footpath juxtaposed against the grass of a natural field.

The information pavilions and shelters may serve varying needs with the passing of time. A structure and external cladding that can be easily expanded, added onto or dispersed was designed in order to accommodate such changes.

**Photographs: Michèle & Miquel**

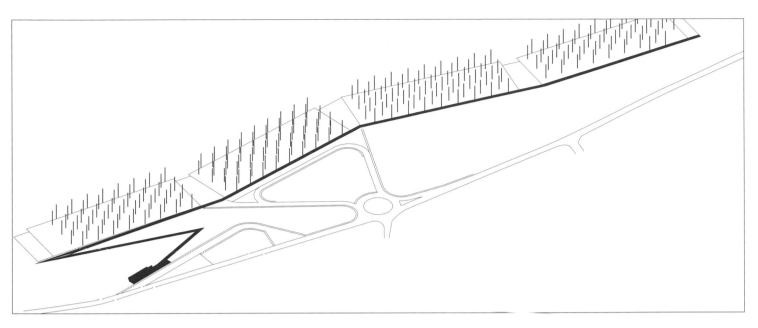

Section, plan and sequence of bus stop

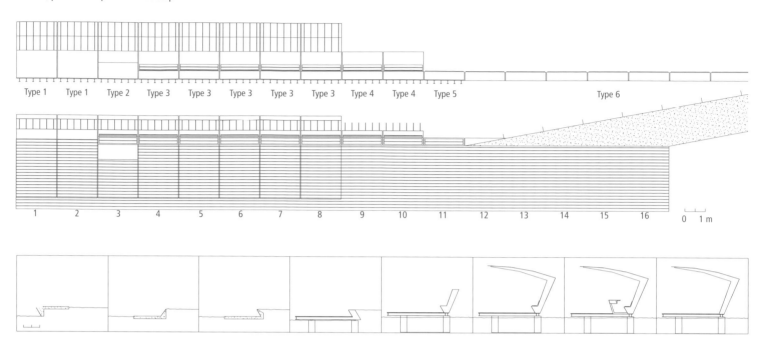

Type 1   Type 1   Type 2   Type 3   Type 3   Type 3   Type 3   Type 3   Type 4   Type 4   Type 5   Type 6

1    2    3    4    5    6    7    8    9    10    11    12    13    14    15    16    0   1 m

Site plan

The high amount of visitors to Les Bulloses in the summer had reached worrying proportions, due to a heightened visual and environmental impact. Orliac Rinuy and Batlle Pagès designed a space with such installations as a 600-vehicle parking lot with 9000 m² of surface area, bus stops, information pavilions and footpaths linking the different components of the complex.

Bus stop. Type 1

Bus stop. Type 2A

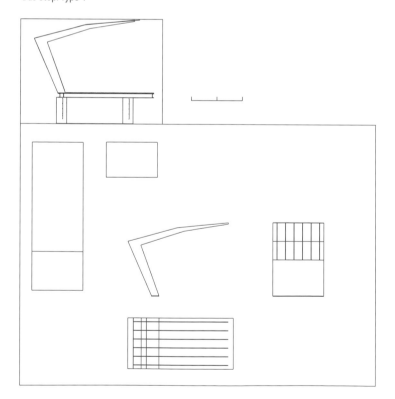
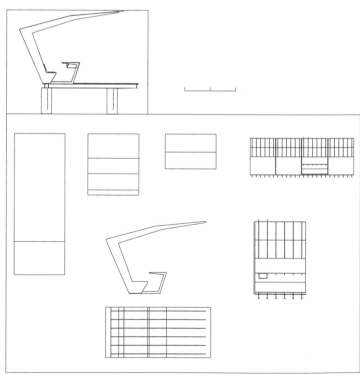

Bus stop. Type 2B

Bus stop. Type 3

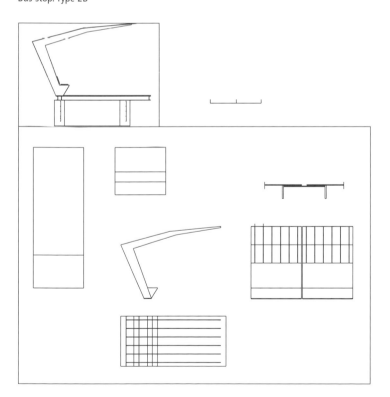

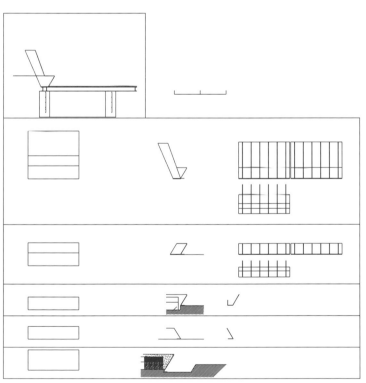

The information pavilions and shelters have been designed to blend in to the forest. Their rough, hermetic exterior skin is made from unpolished wooden slats, which have been pressure-treated with copper salts and fastened together with threaded, galvanized steel bars. This cladding serves at once as structure, sunshade and protection against water, snow and vandalism.

The smooth, translucent interior is done in polycarbonate panels affixed to galvanized steel battens. This surface thermally insulates the interior while also acting as a lining that adheres to wood and, as such, comprises the ceiling, walls, doors, table and shelves. The moving shapes and lights of the exterior landscape are filtered through this interior screen.

Pavilion

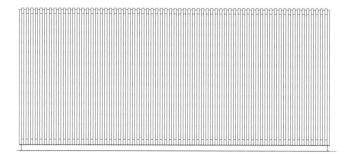

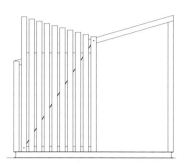

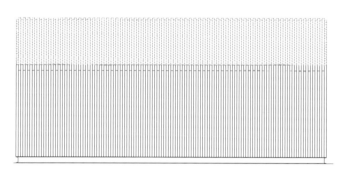

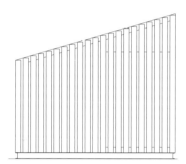

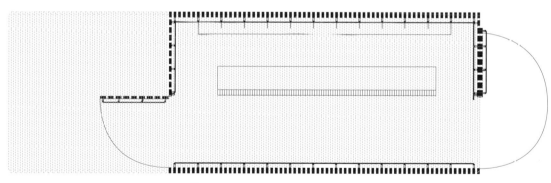

Plan

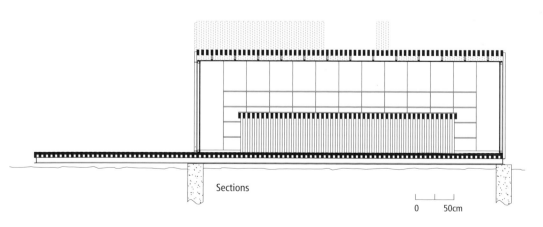

Sections

0    50cm

## Section of pavilion

1. Slat
2. 16x600 mm Danpalon polycarbonate sheet
3. 2Al2 aluminum connector
4. Wooden base slat
5. 8 mm laminated steel tie
6. Neoprene separating layer
7. Bolt and washer
8. Polycarbonate joint sealant, 4PC per panel
9. Stainless Parker screw and washer
10. Wooden paving board
11. Slat treated for flooring
12. Waterproof sheet

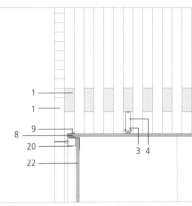

Detail A

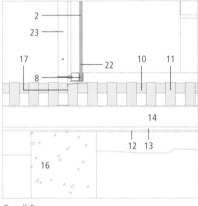

Detail B

0      50cm

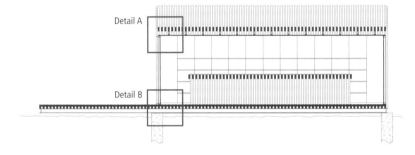

## Plan of pavilion

13. Water-repellent wooden slat
14. IPE-160 steel profile
15. UPE-160 steel profile
16. 100 cm concrete foundation in resistant flooring
17. Galvanized steel or aluminum piece
18. Wooden slat for door
19. Polycarbonate plug, aluminum connector
20. #50 galvanized steel tube doorframe
21. Galvanized steel swivelling door axis
22. Galvanized steel doorskin
23. Stainless steel tie
24. Stainless steel pull

Detail C

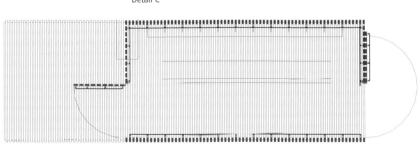

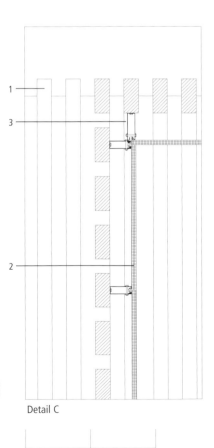

Detail C

0      50cm

Construction details

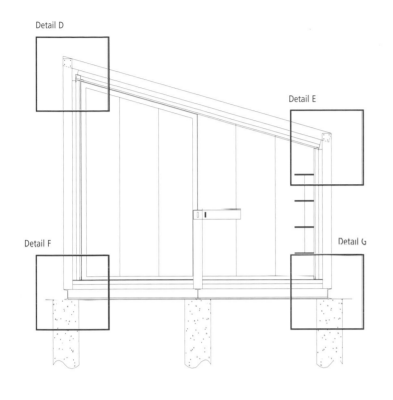

Detail D

Detail E

Detail F

Detail G

Detail D

5
17 7
6
1
2
3
4
1

Detail E

1
2 3 4
5
1
8
4

Detail F

1
2
6
5
8
10
11
14
15
12 13
16

Detail G

3
2
8
10
11
5

[

## Topotek 1
# Postindustrial Park
Eberswalde, Germany

Rolling mill, farriery, ironworks – the industrialization of Land Brandenburg began in Eberswalde by the Finow Canal nearly 200 years ago. Today, ribbons of steel run through the terrain, marking the transformation of an early industrial area into a landscaped park.

Topotek's concept for a post industrial landscape park focuses less on heightening the experience of "industrial romanticism", and more on mapping the site, offering orientation. This does not mean, however, that you cannot experience the industrial past here, taking an underground boat ride along a canal in the old rolling mill for instance. Or enjoying the view from "Montage Eber", a crane which is a landmark of the local industrial tradition.

Equipped with a platform, the meaning and value of this monument from the industrial past are conveyed into the present. From 28 meters above the ground, a magnificent view encompasses the Finow Valley, the site of the Landesgartenschau and the central element of the park, a strip of gardens.

This strip, measuring 50x300 m, is composed of rectangular theme gardens of approximately 150 m² each. They are the showcases of the horticultural exhibition, each displaying a small world of its own. But taken as a whole, the gardens form a unity in the symmetrical layout of an elongated rectangle. An object of deliberate artificiality, full of flowering and scents, incessantly subject to change. It grows into a vibrant architecture that creates permanent changes in the relationships be-

tween each garden. The bold design of the garden strip gains its striking effect especially in contrast to the expanse of the wooded valley around it, a vista that was re-established for the horticultural show.

The second main idea of the design scheme includes the entirety of the former industrial site: a system of paths "mapping" the post industrial park.

40-centimenter-wide steel bands run through the terrain describing wide radii, most of them accompanied by paths. The steel bands span the whole of the new park like the geographical map grid virtually spreads across the globe, made up of meridians and parallels. The lines originate in the proximity of the old rolling mill, thus making them appear to be a product of the former steel production.

These bands define and highlight the expanse of the terrain that was shaped and re-shaped by the old industrial works in the course of their history. By introducing these guiding data, the design scheme accentuates history and simultaneously creates a fresh new experience.

What is extant on site, however, does not get forced into a hierarchy or specific spatial order, but is simply connected by a dynamic grid. The sculptural quality of a former waste disposal site, which was deliberately addressed as an alien element, was heightened by bordering it with a bed of roses of ten meters' width.

**Photographs: Hanns Joosten**

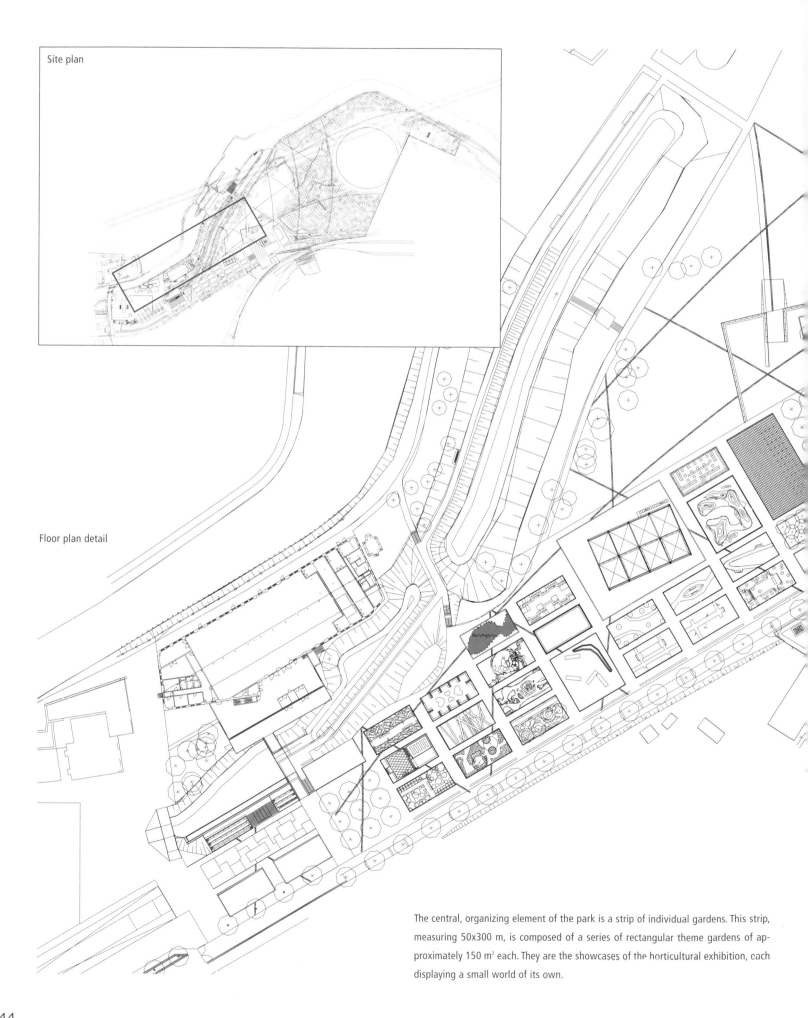

Site plan

Floor plan detail

The central, organizing element of the park is a strip of individual gardens. This strip, measuring 50x300 m, is composed of a series of rectangular theme gardens of approximately 150 m² each. They are the showcases of the horticultural exhibition, each displaying a small world of its own.

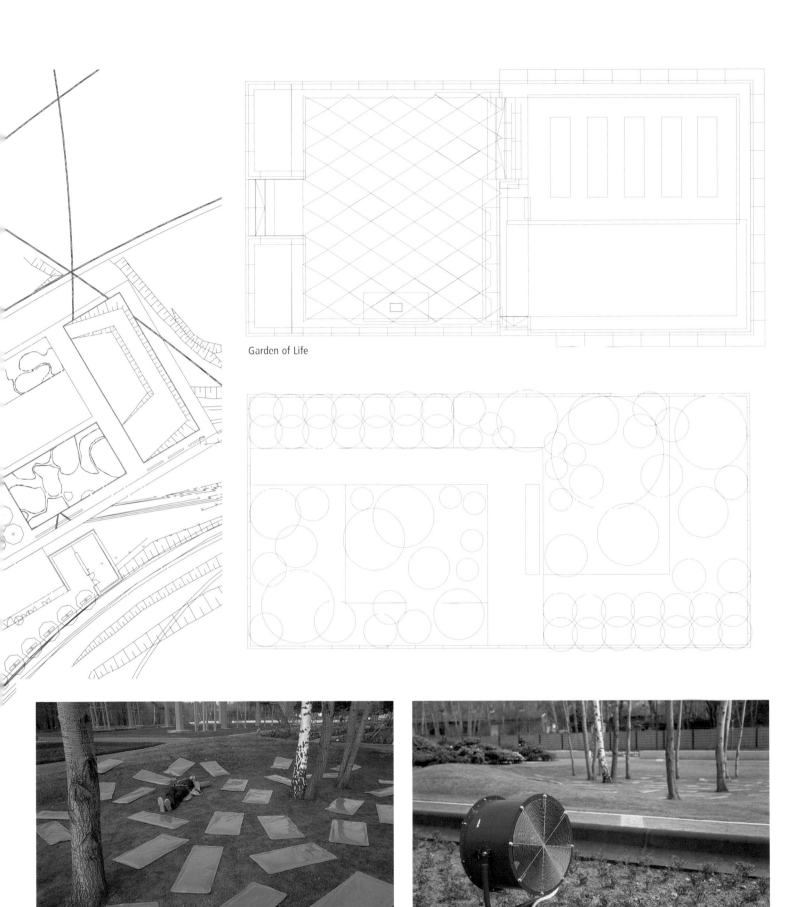

Garden of Life

Lovers' Garden

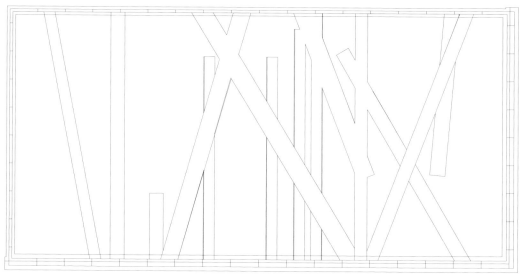

Daniel's Garden

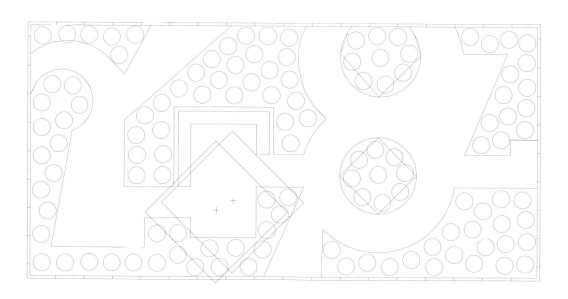

46

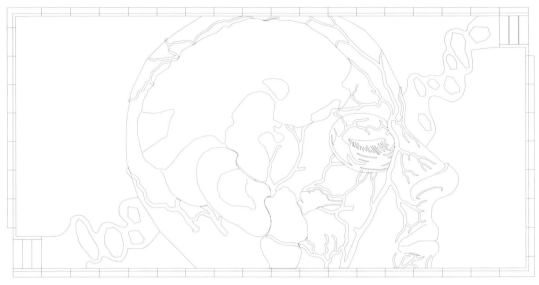

Garden of the Senses

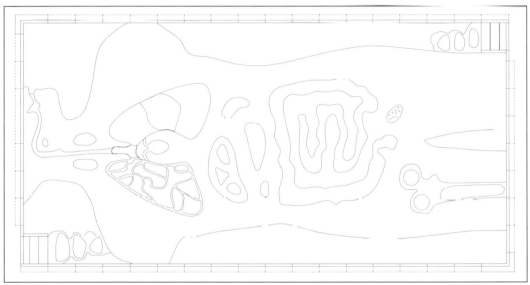

Medicinal Garden

In just three years, 17 hectares of land adjacent to the Finow Canal, a former industrial site dating from the early 19<sup>th</sup> century, were cleared and converted into an innovative park. The park has been given a unique design, lavishing details ranging from picturesque settings on Schleuseninsel Island to the urban graphics on a tarmac square in front of the new stage.

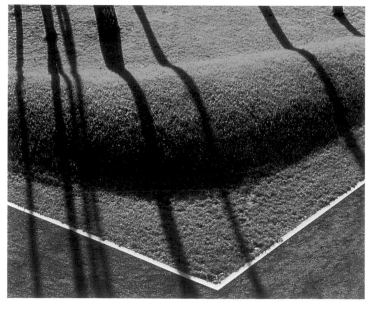 

40-centimenter-wide steel bands run through the terrain describing wide radii, most of them accompanied by paths. The steel bands span the whole of the new park just as the geographical map grid virtually spreads across the globe, made up of meridians and parallels. The lines originate in the proximity of the old rolling mill, thus making them appear to be a product of the former steel production.

## Claudi Aguiló & Isidre Santacreu
### Parc Els Pinetons
Ripollet del Vallès, Spain

The Parc Els Pinetons, conceived as a metropolitan park, sits on a site located at the northernmost tip of the town of Ripollet, on a raised parcel of land that enjoys privileged views of the Marina mountain range, the Montcada valley and peak, the Collserola mountain range, the River Ripoll and the mountain of Montserrat. On a total surface area of 22.7 hectares, the project is restricted to 3 hectares.

The project involved the construction of a footpath surrounding the park and linking a series of 8x55 m platforms intended for varying uses, such as barbecues and play areas for children. Among these platforms is a beverage stand/bar that serves the barbecue area and, in general, adds more life to this phase of the program.

All the volumes have been patterned in the style of the "Havana" beverage stand, which has been built with a structure of steel profiles covered in stratified, phenol-treated sheets. Two zinc pergolas measuring 10 m² each have been included as a terrace in front of the bar.

The general lighting in the park consists of a series of 25-meter-high posts with 14 projectors per column, reinforced by the "area" model beacon. Around the drinks stand, lighting has been built into the pergolas themselves.

The park has been designed with the intention of highlighting a gradation in the degree of "naturalness" between the urban and natural environment. Almost all of the first phase (encompassing the public face which finds its limit at the urban space) is within the apparently most manipulated and artificial part of the park, as opposed to its forest-like surroundings, where pine, oak and cypress mingle. The vegetation lining the ramps, following the alignment of the lampposts, comprises saplings and mature trees, cherry trees, plums and red valerian.

**Photographs: Pau Guerrero**

Site plan

0    50    100m

With this phase of the project begins the footpath surrounding the park, a double surface treatment of asphalt accompanied in places by a "green beach", which enables unlimited use of all of the spaces, without having to renounce the greenery so necessary in a park. All of the volumes have been patterned after the style of the "Havana" beverage stand, which consists of a structure of steel profiles and two 10 m² zinc pergolas used as a terrace for the bar.

General sections

Almost all of the first phase (encompassing the public face which finds its limit at the urban space) is within the apparently most manipulated and artificial part of the park, as opposed to its forest-like surroundings, where pine, oak and cypress mingle. The vegetation lining the ramps, following the alignment of the lampposts, comprises saplings and mature trees, cherry trees, plums and red valerian.

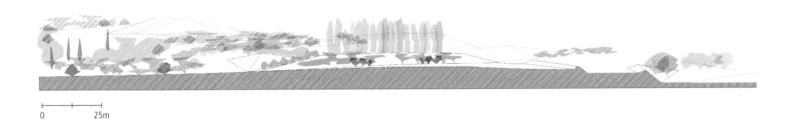

0     25m

## Agence Ter .de
# Landesgartenschau "Aqua Magica 2000"
Bad Oeynhausen and Loehne, Germany

The water park at Bad Oeynhausen, where an imaginary dragon spouts water at random intervals, makes dramatic and varied use of this natural resource. The program, which is the product of a design competition, consisted of the creation of a theme park situated on the outskirts of Bad Oeynhausen and Loehne (near Hanover). The underlying idea behind the program was the search for a new "magical" use for the region's natural springs in order to complete their traditional role in thermal cures – a role which was in clear decline.

Although some of the initial ideas for the project have been temporarily put on hold, the central theme is spectacular enough in its own right. A footpath, lined by gabionades, from which water vapor seeps, leads from the center of Bad Oeynhausen to the park following the fault lines of the terrain. Notches of one to two meters have been cut into the ground, revealing the underground strata, from where the springs originate.

A series of water gardens –the first featuring a playful design and intended for children, the second covered in water plants– have been sunken into troughs preceding the huge crater, which is the park's symbolic and visual centerpiece.

After crossing the third sunken garden, which has been planted with saplings, corten steel stairs lead visitors along walls formed by gabionades and down to the lowest level, five meters below, where a platform encircles the dark waters of a 20 meter deep basin. Water vapor continuously seeps from the walls, while jets of water sporadically shoot from the earth's entrails, controlled by sophisticated technology and accompanied by rumbling sounds and flashing lights.

Following the example of the Chaumont-sur-Loire garden festival, the project was recently expanded to include 300 m² of permanent and temporary gardens on plots provided by both municipalities. Their artificiality has been emphasized by edging the 500-meter-long esplanade with corten steel supporting walls. This "avenue of world climate" leads into fields planted with swaths of grass in varying heights and tones.

**Photographs: Alexandre Petzold**

Site plan

The crater, which is the park's visual centerpiece and which is accessed after passing a series of smaller, sunken gardens, is walled in by gabionades of oxidized sheet metal and stone. The latest addition to the park is a 500-meter-long esplanade lined in corten steel walls that leads into a field planted with a variety of different grass species.

Inside the crater, a misty vapor constantly emanates from the walls. A spiral stairwell of corten steel with perforated metal handrails descends five meters to a platform encircling a pool of water, where a geyser spectacularly erupts at periodic intervals, accompanied by flashing lights and rumblings.

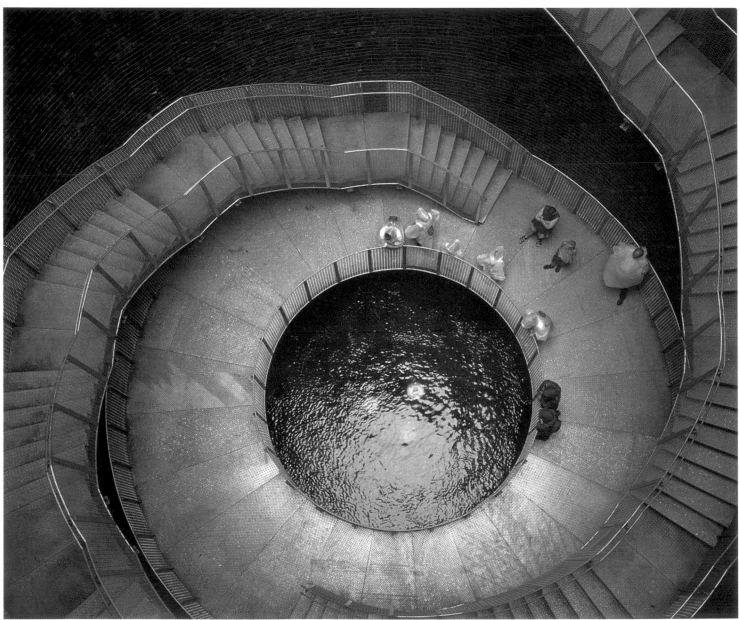

## Expo 02-Swiss National Expo
Yverdon-les-Bains, Switzerland

The "Arteplage", of which the initial theme was human sensuality, at Yverdon-les-Bains was one of the four sites of the Swiss National Exhibition in 2002. Being part of a collaborative design team called "Extasia", West 8 came up with the concept of transforming the grounds of an existing horse-racing track into a spectacular and surreal landscape, a landscape which also establishes a relationship with the lake bordering the site.

Enormous artificial dunes, six meters in height, are the main organizing elements of the design. Wandering between or over these dunes, visitors are confronted with masses of flowers in vibrant colors arranged in psychedelic patterns. The design scheme prescribed only one flower-variety (monoculture) per dune. The profusion of color and design on the dunes is completed on the ground surface by a two-tone gravel pattern.

Various facilities are accommodated in rough, rustic timber structures, which have been integrated into the dunes. These structures act as ar-

tificial body-parts that complete the form of each dune. Each pavilion roof is covered in a translucent material printed with a graphic flower pattern, always mirroring the species on the dune itself.

Media installations enhance the surrealism of this temporary landscape. An artificial, floating cloud forms an objet de desir in the lake of Neuchâtel, accessible only by vanishing into its white foggy substance. Programmatically, the majority of the exhibitions are concentrated in several intersecting buildings with contrasting architectural concepts, one of which integrates, while the other opposes, the landscape. The design of the terrain and its built elements serve to counterbalance the high-tech design of the exhibits themselves.

Because of a natural approach to materials and elementary detailing, every built object on the Arteplage was taken away and recycled afterwards.

**Photographs: Jeroen Musch / West 8**

Labyrinth

Paving: gravel colors

Yellow

Black

On an existing horse-racing track, enormous six-meter-high artificial dunes have been created. Each dune is densely carpeted in a different species of flower arranged in fantastical patterns. This profusion of color and design is completed with two colors of gravel covering nearly the entire exterior ground surface.

**Hill 2 with shops**

South elevation

North/south section

East/west section

**Hill 2**

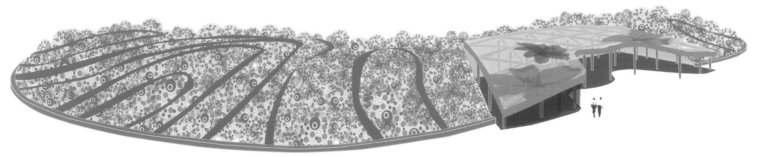

Paving: floor treatment and materials

■ Asphalt

▨ Gravel: 4-20 mm/steamrolled

▨ Gravel: 30-50 mm

▨ Gravel: 80-150 mm

▨ Wood chips

▨ Boardwalk

The design scheme prescribed only one flower-variety per dune. Because of an overall natural approach to materials and elementary detailing, every built object on the Arteplage was removed and recycled after the exhibition.

73

**Hill 3 with restaurant**

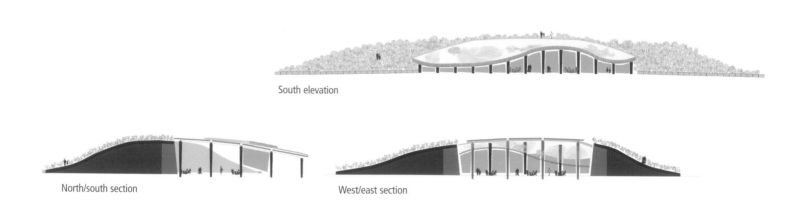

South elevation

North/south section

West/east section

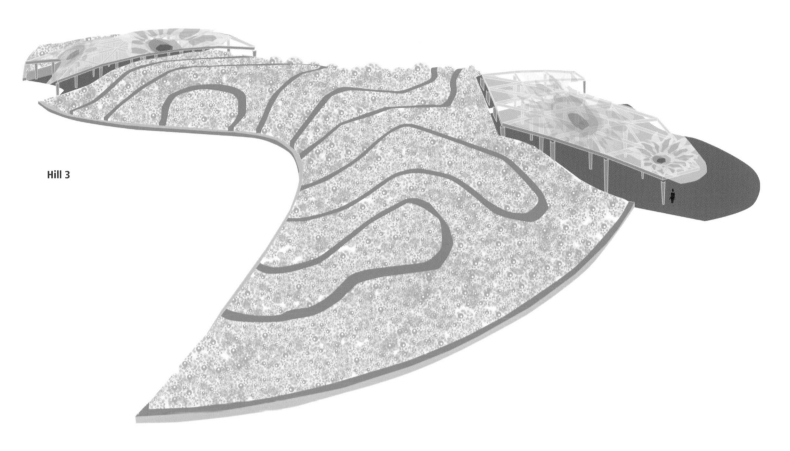

**Hill 3**

Various facilities are housed within rough, rustic timber structures, which have been integrated into the dunes. These structures act as artificial body parts that complete the form of each dune. Each pavilion roof is covered with a translucent material printed with a graphic flower pattern, always mirroring the species on the dune itself.

**Hill 4 with food court**

East elevation

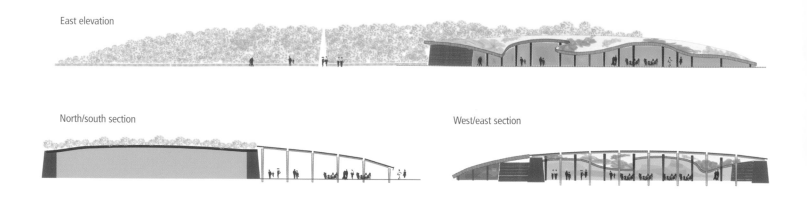

North/south section

West/east section

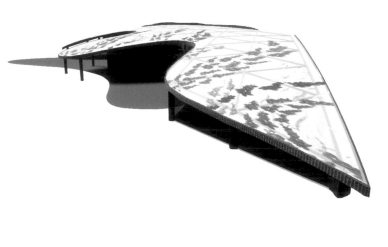

# Sund Garden
Malmö, Sweden

This garden is situated on a landfill at the southern tip of Sweden, where the salty seashore faces Denmark and the new bridge spans the Sund. Here, the rhythm of the tide, the strange waves of the undercurrent and the ice and fog loom large in the Scandinavian and European imagination. This is a place steeped in myth, poetry and song. Decidedly, this is the place for a garden.

The Sund Garden is meant to be a garden in its pure sense: small, enclosed, non-functional and formed on illusions. What seems to be a strange wooden construction from a distance is in fact an enclosed garden. The rectangular garden is framed by a 2.5 m high wall of tree trunks such as the sort of stacked piles waiting to be transported to the mill that one finds in the forest.

Through a gap one enters the garden of "pick-up-sticks", long tree trunks randomly stacked and connected. Hundreds of wildly scattered pine trees in chaotic profusion fill the garden. Was it the result of a storm, an explosion or did it just fall from the sky? Underneath the trees, a carpet of needles, small shrubs and blueberries grow.

This small Swedish forest has an absolute, defined perimeter. All the trees seem decisively cut with mathematical precision to fill a rectangular prism. These cuts have been painted red as well, a color that evokes the wooden houses one finds on the Swedish West Coast. This surreal forest looks and smells like the forest of people's imaginations, the forest from their childhood, the wilderness that covers most of Sweden. The place is wonderfully focused and introverted. There is no view to the landscape, no horizon.

A hidden ladder leads to the roof. Those who climb it through the trees, emerging through an opening in the roof, find themselves in a narrow wooden corridor. Standing on tiptoes, craning over the high plank wall, they find an amazing panorama over the Sund. In the foreground, an undulating shell-covered surface with a number of large smooth rocks merges with the horizon. This suspended shell garden reflects the ocean floor.

**Photographs: Jeroen Musch / West 8**

The rectangular garden is framed by a 2.5 m high wall of tree trunks resembling those stacked piles of logs waiting to be transported to the mill that are often seen in forests. Through a gap one enters the garden of "pick-up-sticks", long tree trunks randomly stacked and connected, hundreds of wildly scattered pine trees fill the garden and are ingeniously propped up so as to support a large square platform.

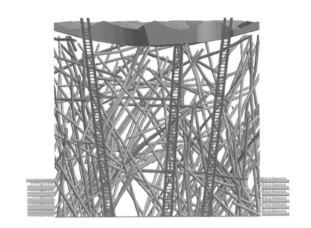

A steep ladder leads to the roof. After climbing through an opening in the roof, visitors find themselves in a narrow wooden corridor. Standing on tiptoes, craning over the high boarding, they are treated to an amazing panorama over the Sund. In the foreground, an undulating surface covered in mussel shells, with a number of large smooth rocks, is a representation of the ocean floor.

## Claudio Vekstein
# Paseo de la Costa del Río de la Plata

Municipio de Vicente López, Argentina

From Amancio Williams' monument, the Paseo de la Costa comprises a permanent large-scale public landscaping encompassing one kilometer of length along the banks of the Río de la Plata in artificially reclaimed terrain and 18 hectares of total surface area, including the Anfiteatro de la Costa (the Coastal Amphitheater).

The project is spread out across a series of geometrically and individually laid out soil and grass embankments, beginning at the monument and stretching southward along the road on one side and, on the other, the winding curve of the river, leaving ample space for a beach of fine silt and abundant riverside vegetation.

Concrete footpaths strewn with benches and street lamps (with inclined fluorescent tubes atop vertical posts) wind their way amidst the embankments, enjoying views of the horizon along the way.

Three openings at the point where these paths meet amongst the embankments give rise to ample parking surfaces with islands of vegetation. The road organizes traffic flow (of vehicles, pedestrians and cyclists) through a combination of dimensions, textures and colors in the layout of the paving, delimiting the outer edges, which in turn serve as organizational tools via dimension, texture, density and color, and a series of different species of autochthonous grass.

At the other end, a continuous line of lampposts rise up like the necks of giraffes, dividing the public park from the restrooms and future concession stands, which will be delimited in dimension and height by the street and the parking lot.

Restrooms are included along the walkway, creating a small public square. Each one features two unequal interior volumes with terraces enjoying views of the walkway.

The route culminates almost naturally at the Anfiteatro de la Costa to the southeast, embracing on the other side the mouth of the Holmberg watercourse and, with the street, looking for its meeting point with the parking lot abutting the children's playground.

The Amphitheater occupies an approximate total ground space of six hectares and is in full relation of continuity with the raised end of the embankments of the walkway itself, raising them still more so as to be able to have space for up to 30,000 spectators.

In Vekstein's words "the proposal for this leg of the Paseo de la Costa alongside the Monument and the Amphitheater is formulated as a movement "from Monument to Non-ument = Foundation", that is, from the "monument" as a symbolic and commemorative structure in its positive, prominent, figurative and vertical form (the pedestal as intermediary between placement and representational sign), to its modern antithesis, as in the case of the monument to Williams, negative in terms of location, as abstract representation of its very autonomy or the landscape that finally adopts it."

**Photographs: Sergio Esmoris, Claudio Vekstein,
Luis Etchegorry, Alessandro Desogos, Sergio Sabag &
Michelo Guzzo**

Site plan

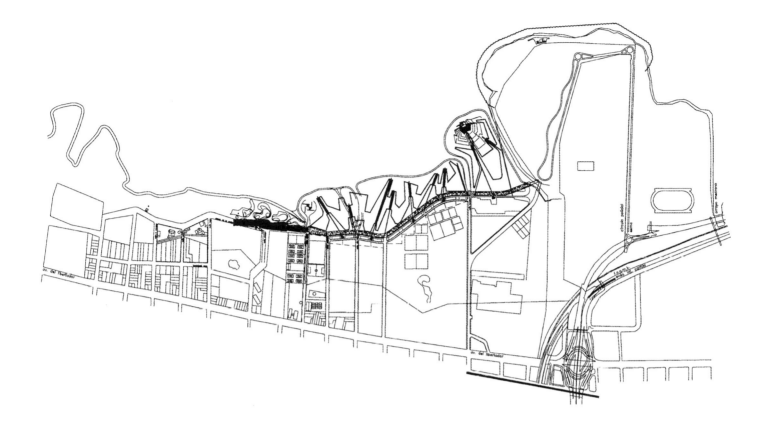

General plan

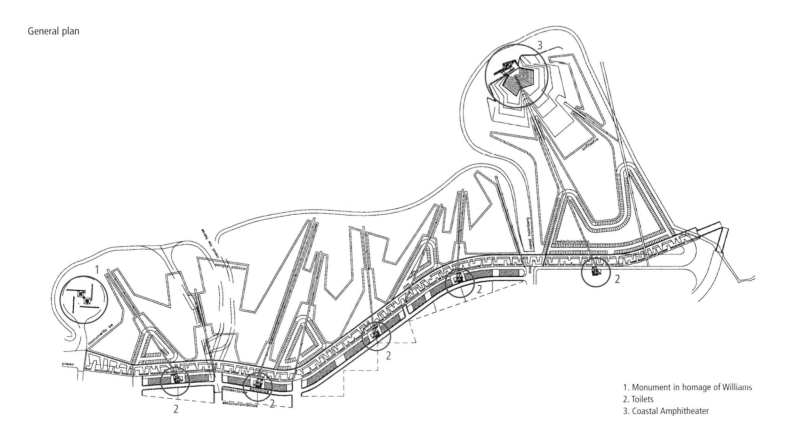

1. Monument in homage of Williams
2. Toilets
3. Coastal Amphitheater

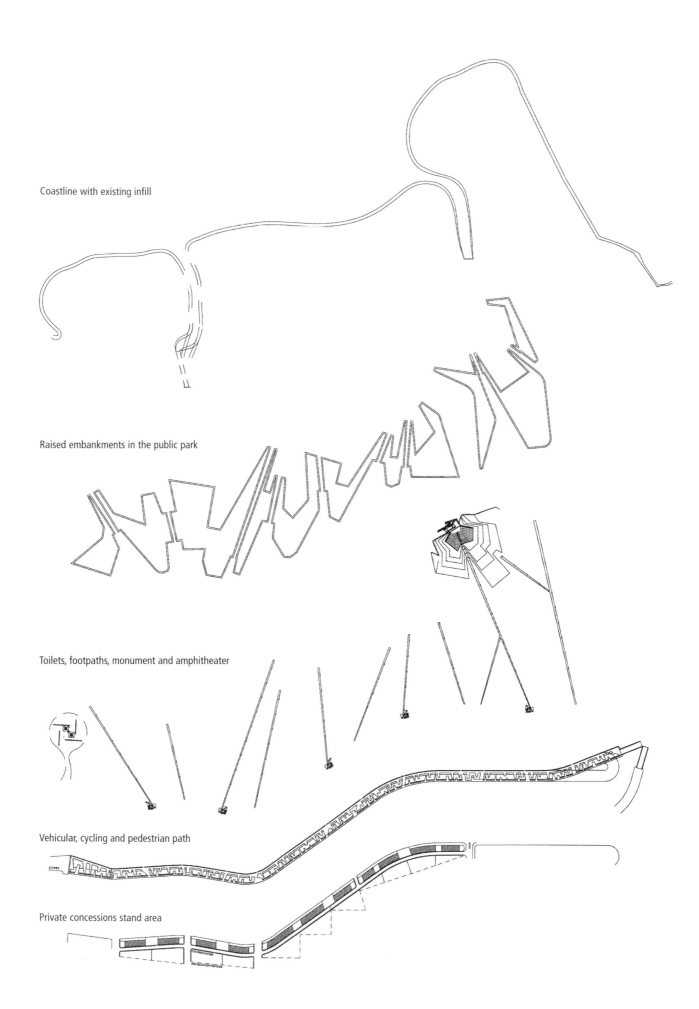

Coastline with existing infill

Raised embankments in the public park

Toilets, footpaths, monument and amphitheater

Vehicular, cycling and pedestrian path

Private concessions stand area

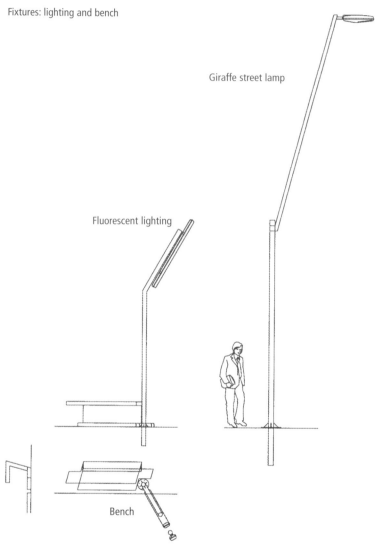

Fixtures: lighting and bench

Giraffe street lamp

Fluorescent lighting

Bench

Detail of placement of the path's interwoven blocks

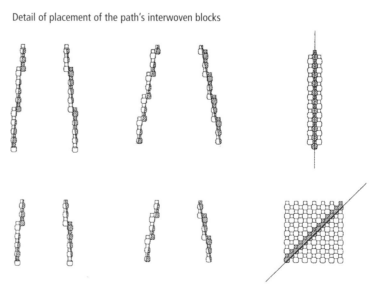

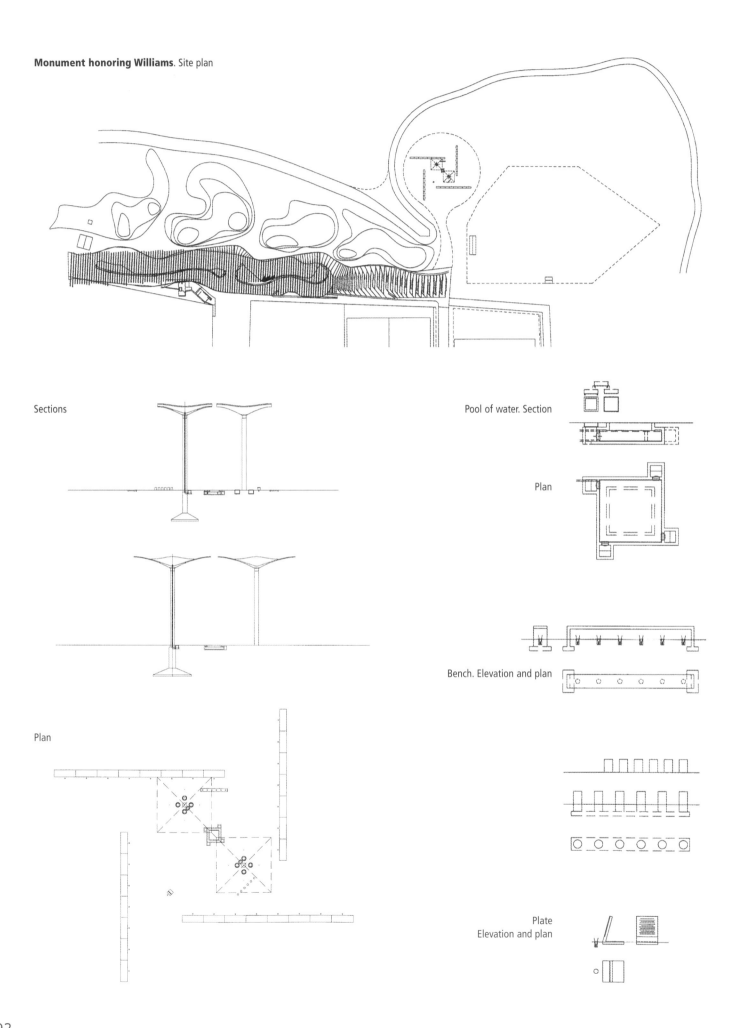

**Monument honoring Williams**. Site plan

Sections

Pool of water. Section

Plan

Plan

Bench. Elevation and plan

Plate
Elevation and plan

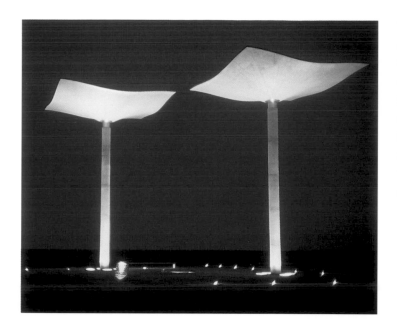

The monument by Amancio Williams (partial reconstruction and adaptation done by Amancio Williams in homage to his father Alberto Williams in 1963) consists of two reinforced concrete quadrangular cul-de-fours, each supported by a single column over an expanse of lawn. Four wide concrete paths lead outward from here toward the surrounding park. The vaults do not touch; rather, their corners are just barely separated, creating a sense of tension in the views from below. A pool of water below reflects the tension between sky and earth, and absorbs the acoustic reflection from the river, which is bounced off the curvature of the vaults.

The public facilities are laid out so as to create small raised public squares. Each facility consists of two unequal internal volumes and, outside, a terrace.

Elevations of toilet facilities

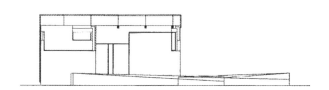

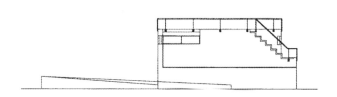

0    4 m

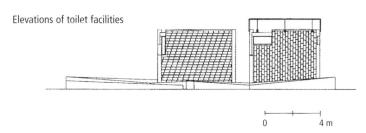

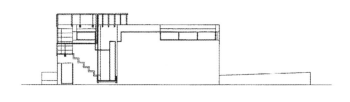

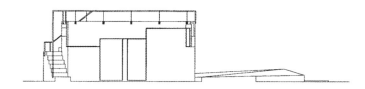

Roof plan

Plan

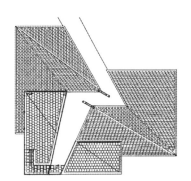

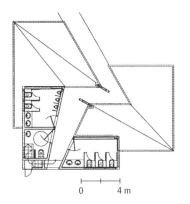

0    4 m

95

Plan and sections of amphitheater

The Amphitheater occupies an approximate total ground area of six hectares and is in full relation of continuity with the raised end of the embankments of the walkway itself, raising them still more so as to be able to have space for up to 30,000 spectators. Thus, varying levels in relatively concentric sectors arise in relation to the stage. Abutting this is a large parking lot with islands of vegetation, beyond which are three large "hills", like embankments, descending toward the river.

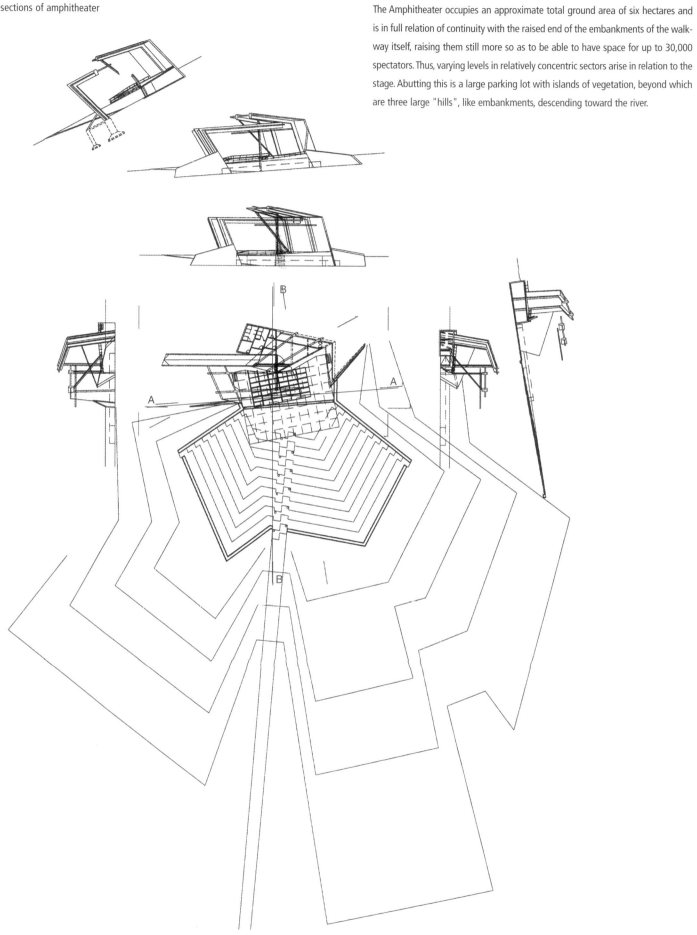

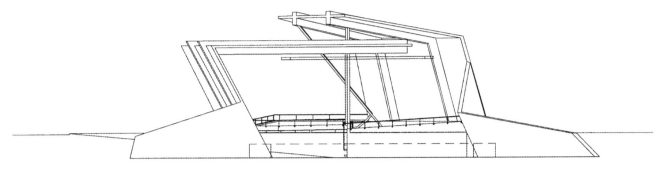

Elevation AA

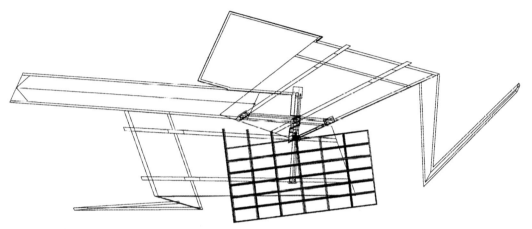

Upper plan

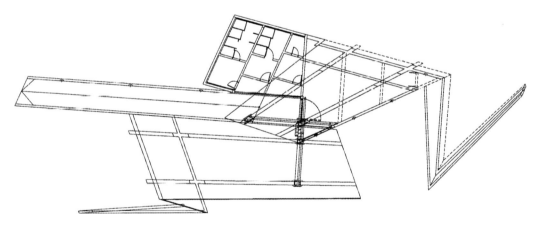

Lower plan

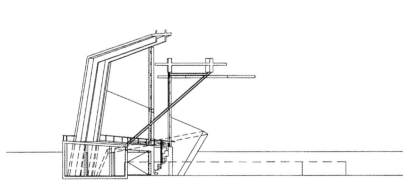

Section BB

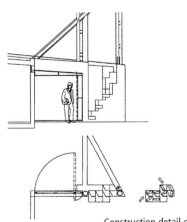

Construction detail of stairs

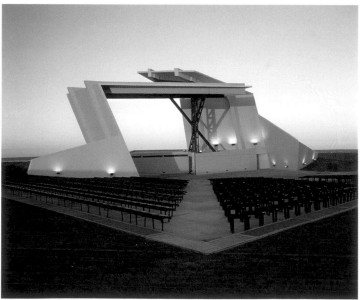

The seating area of the Amphitheater is made up of a reinforced concrete surface that is barely striated by the minimal terracing, divided into two large sectors by the path leading from the entrance. The stage provides performance space of up to 15x20 m, accessed via an exterior ramp.

The dressing rooms, toilets and storehouse are covered by a tilted slab that serves as choir and possible extension of the stage. Partially covering the stage area are two large roof panels – one perfectly horizontal and aligned with the river, the other tilted and almost resting on the first. Both are supported by pairs of columns, which are in turn composed of double steel beams, one vertical and the other inclined.

## Miguel Centellas, Olga Tarrasó, Julià Espinàs & Teresa Galí
# Parque de la Alpujarra
Berja, Spain

This was the winning proposal in a competition for a project on the Cerro (hill) de La Mohaja on an approximate surface area of 8 hectares, although in a preliminary phase only 2.8 hectares were dealt with. The topography was a decisive element in the projected work, as a difference in level of 55 meters had to be bridged.

The winning plan was simple: to adapt the layout to the orography of the hill, on which a gently curving path with an 8% slope led toward the peak, which enjoys splendid views of the Sierra Nevada. Along the way, certain routes had been cut off, making design of the park's footpaths somewhat more difficult.

The site's topographical aspects guided the general structure conferred upon the space. A more extensive flat area occupies the lower part of the plot and lies alongside Alpujarra Avenue, while a series of platforms hugging the slope make use of rows of former terraced farming beds, achieving maximum integration into the landscape with a minimum of effort.

The watering system was optimized by using the park's own hydric resources. Particular attention was paid to the design of the runoff basins. Rainwater is channeled through gutters running alongside the path toward their final destination in tanks beneath the terraces. The levels immediately below are watered by runoff, complementing the watering system and economizing the water supply.

The exigencies of a tight budget combined with the demand for easy maintenance necessitated the almost exclusive use of concrete with two surface treatments. In the square at the entrance, a set retardant enabled the final layer of cement paste to be washed, resulting in a concrete with a smooth aggregate finish. In the upper square, the surface has been polished to give it an exposed aggregate finish. A number of cast in situ concrete tiers serve as a backdrop to this platform.

The highest containing walls are of reinforced concrete clad in dry laid stone. The lower ones are made from material resulting from the excavation and have been finished in stone, recalling the texture of the walls of the terraced plots and easing integration into the existing landscape.

The markedly Mediterranean autochthonous vegetation was given priority. Rubber plant was planted in the lower square; almond and hackberry trees grace the terraces, and pine trees line the footpaths and tiers.

The fixtures, such as benches and railings, have been made with strips of autoclave treated pine and affixed flat steel bars.

Lighting systems were included only in the lowest squares, with columns bearing individual lamps (at the entrance) or with various lamps (on the highest). On the rest of the paths, the only lighting consists of ground-level posts to deter vandalism; these posts will one day light the route leading to the summit.

**Photographs: Fernando Alda**

The highest containing walls are of reinforced concrete clad in dry laid stone. The lower ones are made from material resulting from the excavation and have been finished in stone, recalling the texture of the walls of the terraced plots and easing integration into the existing landscape.

Site plan and garden

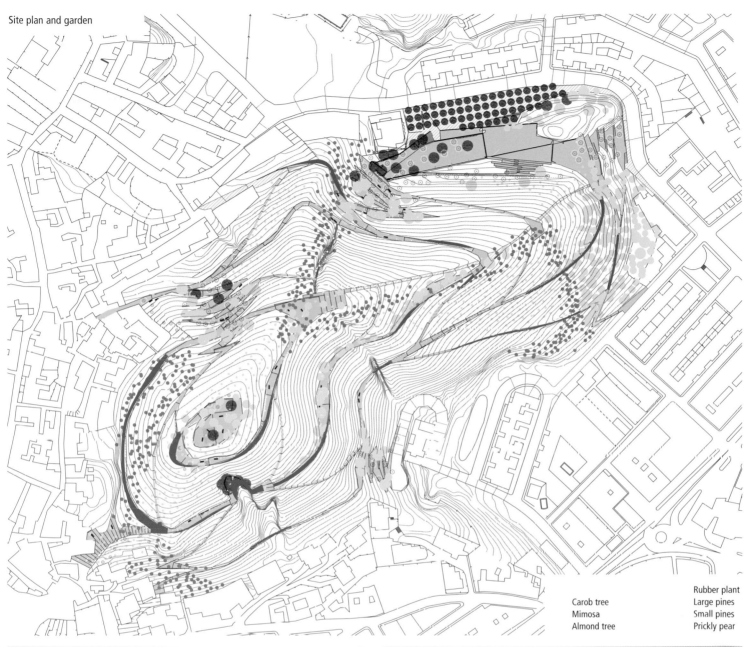

Carob tree
Mimosa
Almond tree

Rubber plant
Large pines
Small pines
Prickly pear

103

Section of access ramp onto square

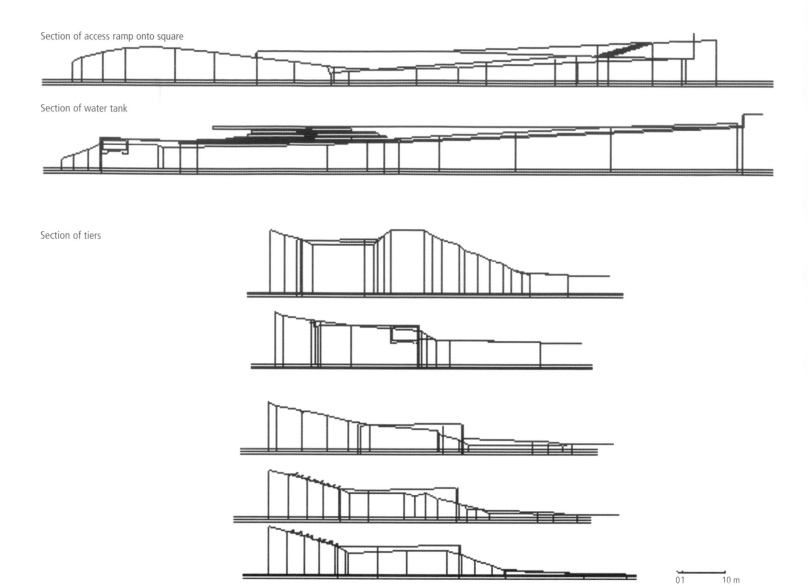

Section of water tank

Section of tiers

01       10 m

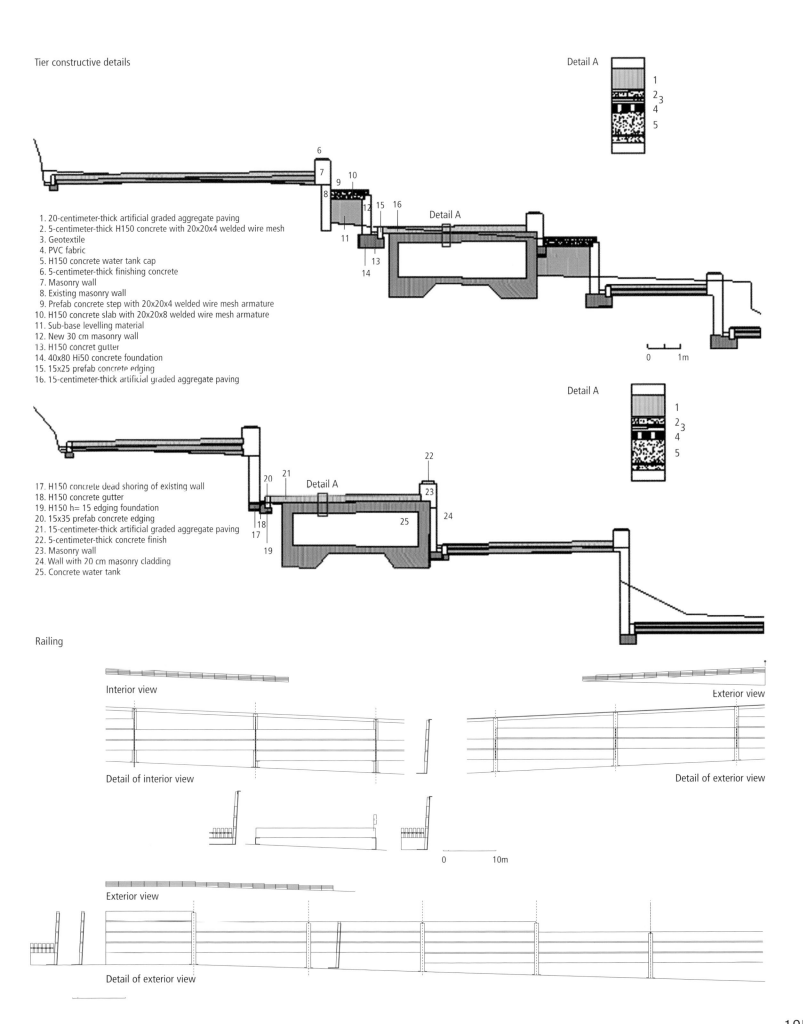

Tier constructive details

Detail A

1. 20-centimeter-thick artificial graded aggregate paving
2. 5-centimeter-thick H150 concrete with 20x20x4 welded wire mesh
3. Geotextile
4. PVC fabric
5. H150 concrete water tank cap
6. 5-centimeter-thick finishing concrete
7. Masonry wall
8. Existing masonry wall
9. Prefab concrete step with 20x20x4 welded wire mesh armature
10. H150 concrete slab with 20x20x8 welded wire mesh armature
11. Sub-base levelling material
12. New 30 cm masonry wall
13. H150 concret gutter
14. 40x80 Hi50 concrete foundation
15. 15x25 prefab concrete edging
16. 15-centimeter-thick artificial graded aggregate paving

0    1m

Detail A

17. H150 concrete dead shoring of existing wall
18. H150 concrete gutter
19. H150 h= 15 edging foundation
20. 15x35 prefab concrete edging
21. 15-centimeter-thick artificial graded aggregate paving
22. 5-centimeter-thick concrete finish
23. Masonry wall
24. Wall with 20 cm masonry cladding
25. Concrete water tank

Railing

Interior view

Exterior view

Detail of interior view

Detail of exterior view

0    10m

Exterior view

Detail of exterior view

105

# Shuhei Endo
## Springtecture H
Harima, Japan

This is a facility in a small park sited in a highly artificial location that can be reached in one hour from Osaka, using the bullet train in the mountains of Hyogo Prefecture, Japan. As a facility for general use, of a kind that can be found anywhere in Japan, it defies expression of any regional character.

Located in a park sandwiched by newly built elementary and secondary school buildings, the facility has a simple structure comprising three sections: a janitor's room, men's toilet and women's toilet. Public lavatories are required to provide convenience (based on openness) and security (requiring a sense of enclosure). This small facility, apparently a simple assemblage of parts, is described as "Halftecture" (half + architecture), since it is characterized simultaneously by being at once open and closed.

Openness is essentially the possibility of passage. In the case of this facility, however, passage is provided in three directions, with no clearly defined entrance. This avoids the defensiveness that is created, paradoxically, by demarcated openings and the transparency of glass; in other words making the whole facility a structure for passage, suggesting the possibility of entrance from almost anywhere.

On the other hand, its closed attribute is created by the use of corrugated steel sheet roofs, walls and floors, to which permeability is added by the 3.2 mm clearance of reversed steel sheets. The structure is basically in the form of an independent spiral of steel sheets, with partially inserted metal bars for support.

The architectural concept of this facility aims to form a linkage between being open and closed through continuity of corrugated steel sheets. Interior walls double as ceilings and floors, which also extend as exterior walls and roofs and once again turn into interior parts. The interior and exterior form a linkage of changes, challenging architectural norms expected by the observer, and suggesting a new, heterogeneous architectural form. The facility is also a small step toward a new architecture realized by continuous interplay between the interior and the exterior and the interactive effect of partial sharing of roofs, floors and walls.

**Photographs: Yoshiharu Matsumura**

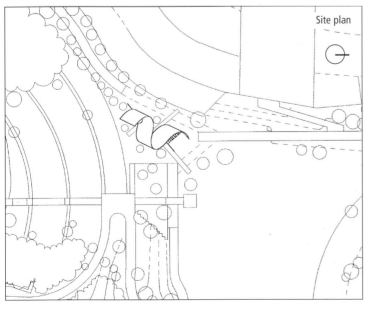

Site plan

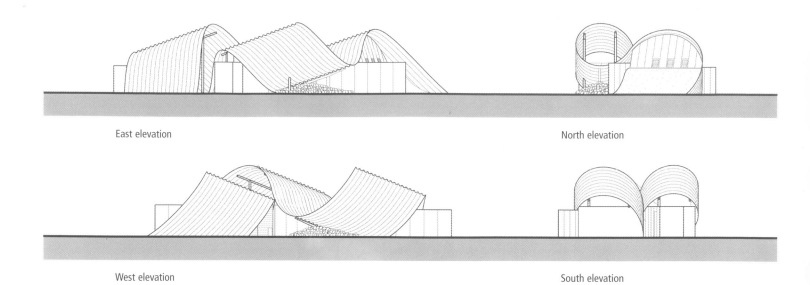

East elevation

North elevation

West elevation

South elevation

Concept of corrugated steel expansion

The building's closed aspect is created by the use of corrugated steel sheet roofs, walls and floors, to which permeability is added by the 3.2 mm clearance of reversed steel sheets. The structure is basically in the form of an independent spiral of steel sheets, with partially inserted metal bars for support.

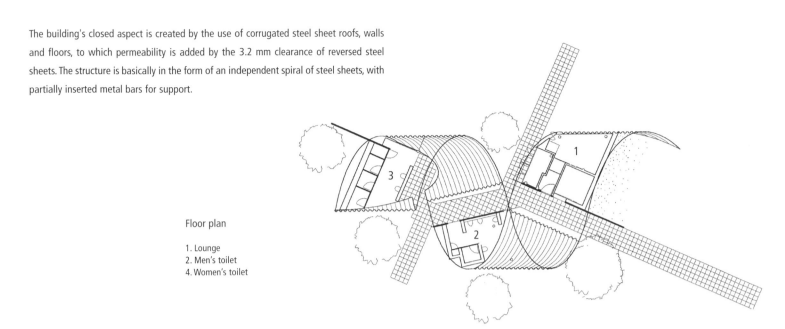

Floor plan

1. Lounge
2. Men's toilet
4. Women's toilet

# The Meadow Park on the Wuhle
Berlin, Germany

This design was the winning proposal in the "Wuhlepark Landsberger Tor" international landscape planning competition (1997) for a site located in the northeast of Berlin, between two large housing estates. The aim of the project was to sculpt the urban periphery through the development of strong landscape structures, consciously highlighting the transitional stage of a space which is no longer rural but also not yet urban.

The transition from the urban space of the housing blocks and its Stadtgarten to the wide open space of the Wuhle Valley, defined by the meadowpark, was formally and prominently staged. The smaller part of the park is the Stadtgarten, which comprised the first construction phase. This elongated urban space is characterized by a prominent, wave-like modulation of the terrain. Special areas for recreation have been embedded into the waves of the lawn.

The vegetation has been specially chosen to characterize each location: shrubs dance along the wave, trees provide shade in the urban spaces and groves serve to demarcate peripheral areas.

The concrete wall clearly borders and thereby marks the lawn wave as a ground sculpture. Chair, bench and wastebasket, as furniture custom designed for this project, characterize the central square. A unique accent is formed by a perennial garden contained by lamella walls.

The waves of the Stadtgarten "flow" directly into the meadowpark, which is the project's second phase. In its expansiveness the new park forms an exciting mixture of natural landscape, artificial "implants" and urban elements. The broad meadow is characterized by individual groups of trees, simple paths and special places that encourage the active appropriation of the park.

Two individual playground designs were developed for the meadowpark. The playground "The Wuhle" is especially designed for small children and evokes the story of a mother whale with her offspring. The design idea for the "Meadow Dream" playground was to create a prominent place which allows older children and adolescents enough free space to develop their own ideas for the completion of the site.

Overall, these are quiet meadow areas with unpretentious spatial design – a point of attraction for multigenerational recreation on the outskirts of Berlin.

**Photographs: A. Muhs, F. Profitlicu, Gruppe F**

Tree plan

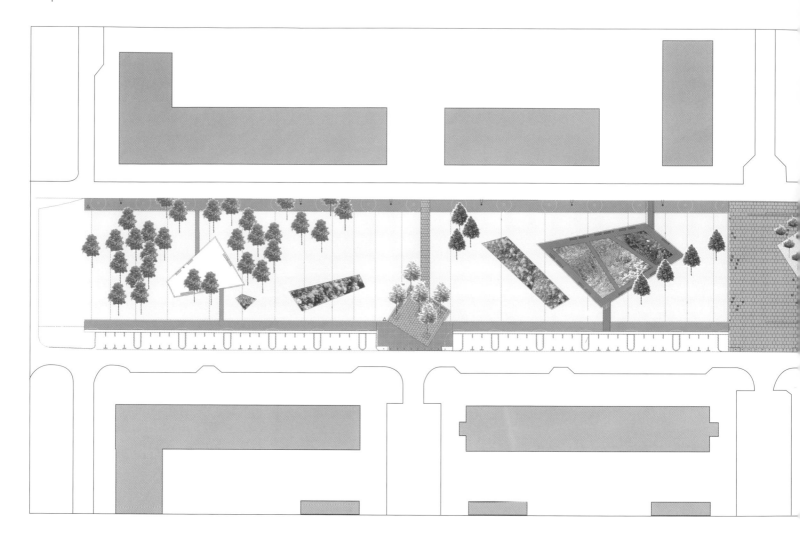

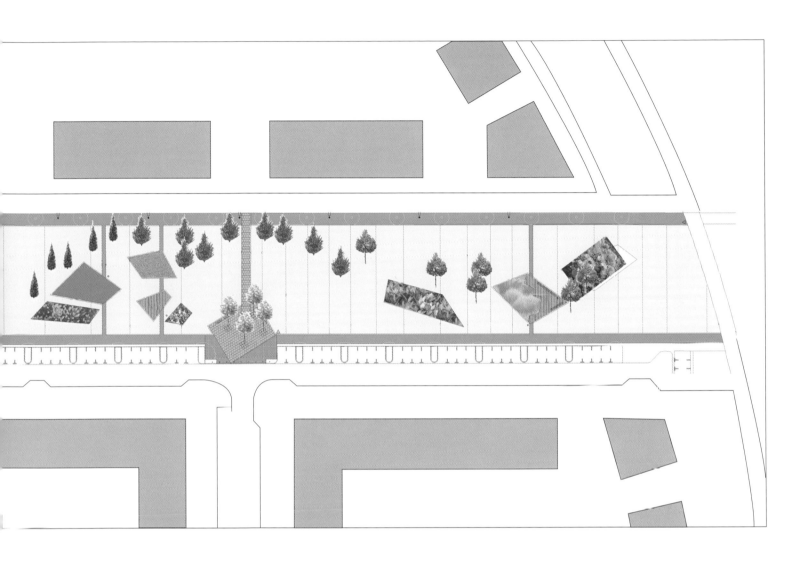

115

Competition ground plan

The contours of the concrete retaining wall accentuate the wave-like curves of the land-scape, into which have been cut open areas of varying sizes to be used for recreational purposes. Vegetation in the park has been specially chosen to characterize each location: shrubs dance along the wave, trees provide shade in the urban spaces and groves serve to demarcate peripheral areas.

Latz + Partner
## Landscape Park Duisburg Nord
Duisburg, Germany

The Landscape Park Duisburg Nord is set on the site of a former blast furnace plant and comprises one of the key projects of the International Building Exhibition in Germany. While water is a central feature of the park, there is no longer any naturally running water on the site, due in part to extensive areas having been sealed off because of hydrocarbon contamination.

The open waste water canal (known as the "Old Emscher") crossing the park from east to west once carried untreated sewage to the Rhine. The profile of this old structure was used when designing a new clean water system in order to avoid contact with the surrounding polluted soil.

All waste water is now carried within an underground conduit of 3.5 meters in diameter. This is encased within a layer of clay, which collects runoff from the buildings and channels it toward the former ore bunkers, cooling ponds and settling tanks. This installation represents the largest investment in the park, costing more than all the other equipment combined.

Rainwater flows in open rivulets, through the existing overhead pipe systems, and is channeled through new pipes, such as those at the old power station, which collect runoff from a roof of approximately 6000 m$^2$ in surface area. It is also gathered in some of the former ore bunkers and cleaned settling tanks, which now serve as retention basins. It falls into the former cooling ponds, becoming enriched by oxygen in the process. Now, water lilies and iris bloom in pure water, and fish and dragonflies live in a new biotope.

This system of open and visible water paths leads through the whole blast furnace site in the direction of the new watercourse, where platforms with seats await visitors and small islands are already colonized by a variety of flora and fauna.

In order to harness the power of the wind for use in an oxygenation system, a windmill was set up in the tower of the former sintering plant. With a diameter of 16 meters, it is the largest rotor in the world of its kind. Water is pumped from the canal through an Archimedean screw and falls from several points after making its way through the gardens.

**Photographs: Latz+Partner, Christa Panick &
Peter Schäfer, Michael Latz.**

## Imma Jansana Ferrer
# Jardines de Àngel Guimerà
El Prat de Llobregat, Spain

These gardens are located in the interior of a block in the old quarter of El Prat de Llobregat (near Barcelona). The site for the project consisted of an empty plot and the grounds of an old, private garden – the former providing access to the latter.

These old, private gardens were filled with a leafy vegetation consisting of various tree species (prunes, figs, laurel, acacia), some of which were particularly interesting because of their sheer size, such as the canary palms. The entire ground surface was covered in a tapestry of acanthus and creepers. This garden had been neglected for some 20 years, during which time the ecosystem was left to its own devices, giving rise to a unique combination of plants. In contrast, the plot facing the main street was entirely empty and free from all plant life.

The architect proposed two very different strategies in her plan. On the one hand, based on the need to keep the flora and the private garden's unique ecosystem intact, she concluded that the only way of conserving it was to create an enclosed garden. Thus, the plan con-

sisted of tidying and pruning the vegetation and installing a number of wooden plank platforms. The idea was to not interfere unduly in the garden's natural development. The growth of the acanthus was particularly encouraged as a good ground cover.

The second part of the proposal turned the empty lot abutting the main street into an entrance to the old garden as well as a small garden in its own right, planted with aromatic plants. This smaller garden was patterned after traditional orchards in the area of the Delta del Llobregat: orchards comprising a network of footpaths bordered by narrow water channels built in brick. The aromatic species chosen were native Mediterranean varieties.

Lastly, a row of cypresses was planted around this secondary garden, forming a sort of hedge which kept the garden of scent and touch a secluded space, independent from the rest of the garden.

**Photographs: Lourdes Jansana**

Former garden of Mr. Roigé
New "touch and smell" garden

General floor plan

Existing tree species

- Ficus Carica
- Eriobotrya Japonica
- Laurus Nobilis
- Citrus Auriantum Var
- Robinia Pseudo-Acacia
- Prunus Doméstica
- Phoenix Canadiensis
- Phoenix Dactylifera
- Punica Granatum
- Cydonia Vulgaris
- Hereda Helix
- Ligustrum Japonicum
- Phoenix Washingtonia
- Pittosporum
- Prunus Pisardi
- Citrus
- Ruscus Acquileatus
- Palmera

Newly planted tree species

- Cupresus Sempervirens
- Berberis Thumbergi Antropurpurea
- Abelia Floribundya
- Marfull
- Ampelopsis
- Herera Helix
- Rapholepis Indica
- Artemisia Absunthum
- Foeniculum Vulgare
- Lavandula Officianalis
- Lavandula Latifolia
- Lavandula Stoechas
- Lavandula Angustifolia
- Rosmarinus Offcianalis
- Salvia Officinalis
- Santolina Chamaecyparissus
- Thymus Serpyllum
- Thymus Vulgaris
- Thymus Citriodora
- Mentha Spicata
- Origanun Vulgare
- Ocinum Basilicum
- Aloysia Thiphylla

Central Street

These old, private gardens were filled with a leafy vegetation consisting of various tree species (prunes, figs, laurel, acacia), some of which were particularly interesting because of their sheer size, such as the canary palms. The entire ground surface was covered in a tapestry of acanthus and creepers. The plan consisted of tidying and pruning the vegetation and installing a number of wooden plank platforms, as well as new fixtures throughout. The empty lot abutting the main street was turned into an entrance to the old garden as well as a small garden in its own right, planted with aromatic plants.

**Detail of the aromatic plant garden**

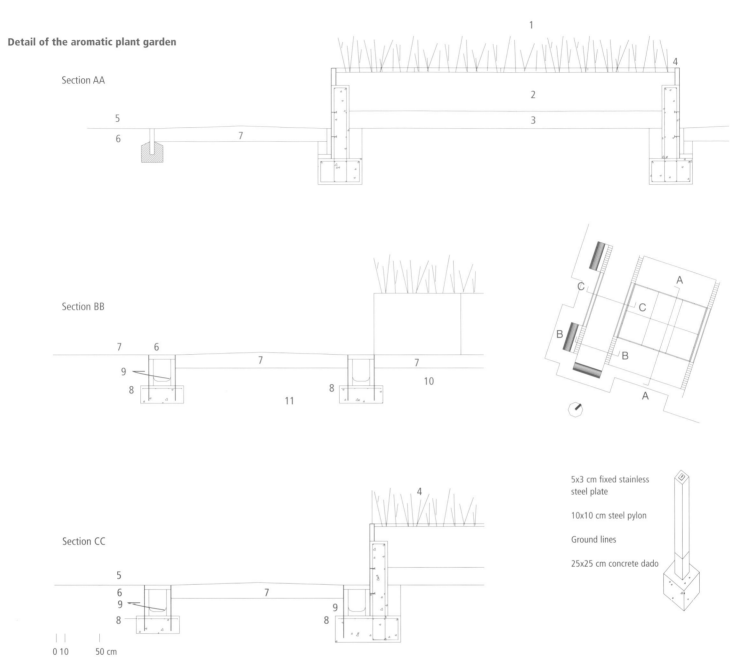

Section AA

1

4

5

2

6

3

7

Section BB

7  6

9

8

7

7

8  10

11

C

C

A

B

B

A

Section CC

5

4

6

9

8

7

9

8

5x3 cm fixed stainless
steel plate

10x10 cm steel pylon

Ground lines

25x25 cm concrete dado

0 10    50 cm

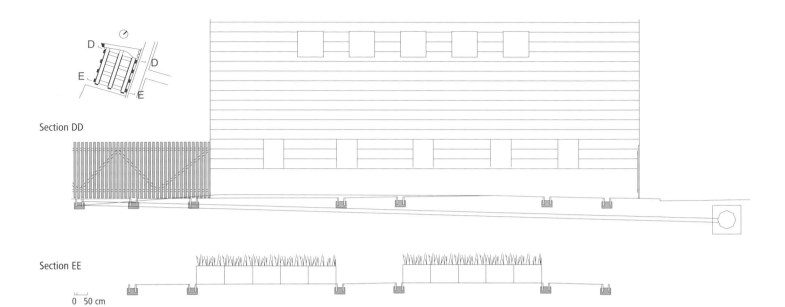

Section DD

Section EE

0  50 cm

1. Aromatic plants
2. Soil mixed with fine sand
3. 4/6 gravel
4. 3 mm folded steel plate
5. Cupresus Sempenviren
6. Soil

7. Feldspathic sand of granite origin
8. Ø 4c15.15 welded wire mesh
9. 5 mm galvanized plate
10. Gravel
11. Concrete footing

The new aromatic plant garden was patterned after traditional orchards from the Delta del Llobregat, with large rectangular plant boxes of 70 cm steel and meandering footpaths bordered by brick water conduits, with smell and touch a constant, immediate presence. The species chosen for the garden were native Mediterranean plants, such as lavender, rosemary, mint, oregano, salvia and maria luisa, for example.

## Jõao Álvaro Rocha
**Parque de Lazer de Moutidos**
Maia, Portugal

Situated in a territory marked by strong tensions between a recently constructed grid, small tree-lined areas and others intended for agricultural
use, the project should have the capacity to generate the difficult equilib-
rium between very different types of occupation, apparently unable to en-
dow structure to the place. This situation is common to the growth of the
territory: rural areas that are slowly being deactivated and substituted by
an occupation that spreads along the main roads without any ordering
method, and without any attention to the treatment of public space.
Confronted with this image, the project should be able to find its place

in its own singularity, not only through the acknowledgement of the
different constructive senses that characterize it, but also through the
way it proposes to stay in the place it wishes to occupy.
In such a complex context the intervention can only find its reason for
being, in the relation it can establish between land and territory, in the
dialogue between constructed forms, between open and closed, between big and small – between man and nature.
The physical boundaries that shape this large precinct are defined
through the use of two distinctive materials, their respective construc-

tion techniques and consequent sensorial perception. They have been organized into two categories corresponding to the two realities that coexist in the territory: that which corresponds to the schools and the residential nucleus set adjacent to the street the park faces; and its rural character, comprised of an agricultural parcel and a large estate.

The precinct is then defined, from two articulated "frames". To the west, along the street, it assumes a more urban character, as if it were a façade, expressing itself in a solid manner, static, heavy and rich in textures. To the east, one boundary element manifests itself in a softer manner, equally uniform, but organic in its extension and landscape continuity and is designated as a "vegetable wall".

The way objects are placed inside this precinct is based on the repetition of a simple element that unfolds to respond to different uses, sometimes made up of small groups, other times dispersed. Their placement is not random; quite the contrary, they are organized in an attempt to establish a punctuation in the territory.

**Photographs: Luis Ferreira Alves**

Site plan

0   60m

Sections of terrain

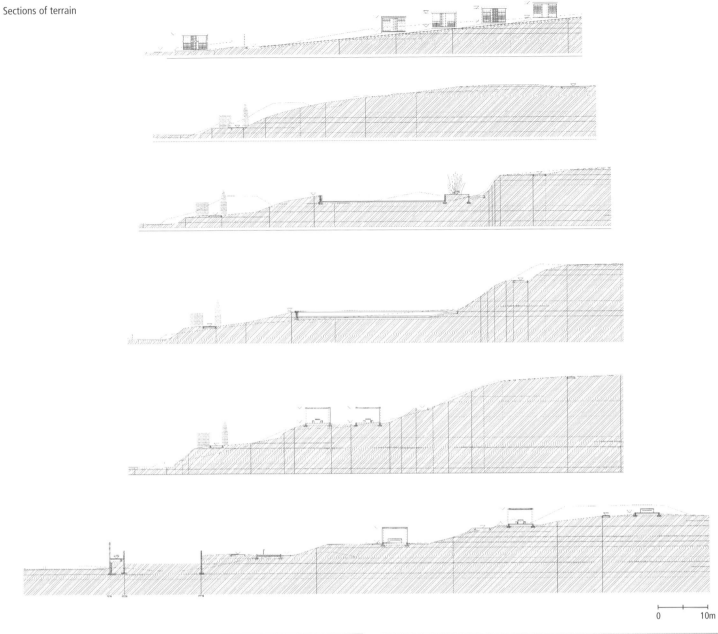

0     10m

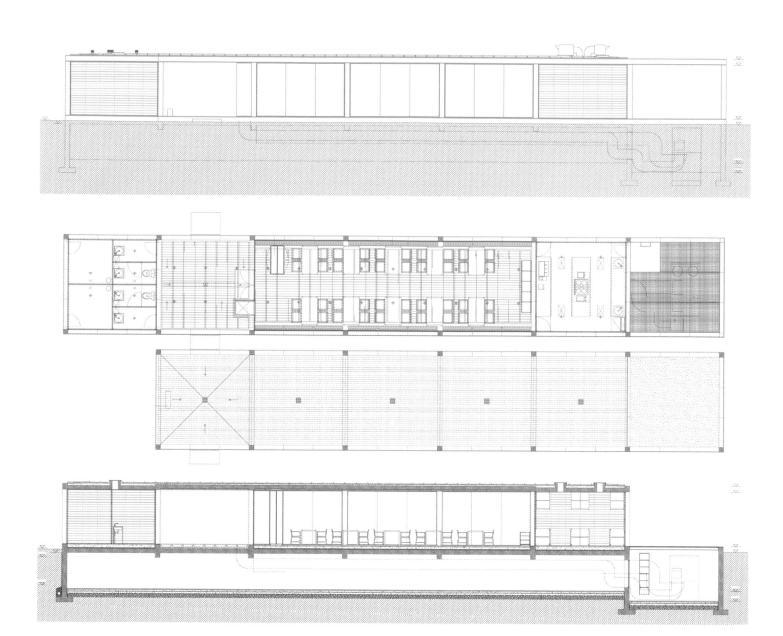

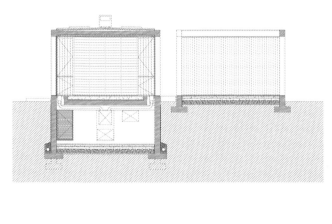
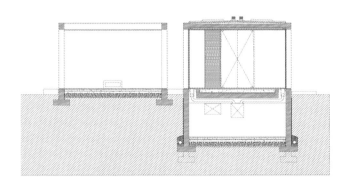
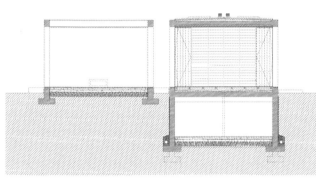
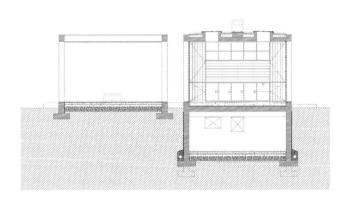
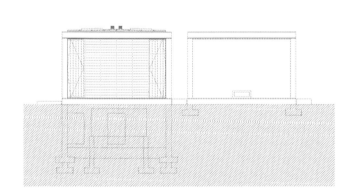
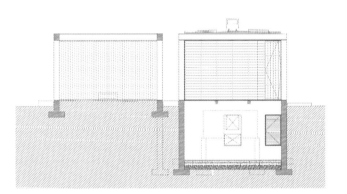

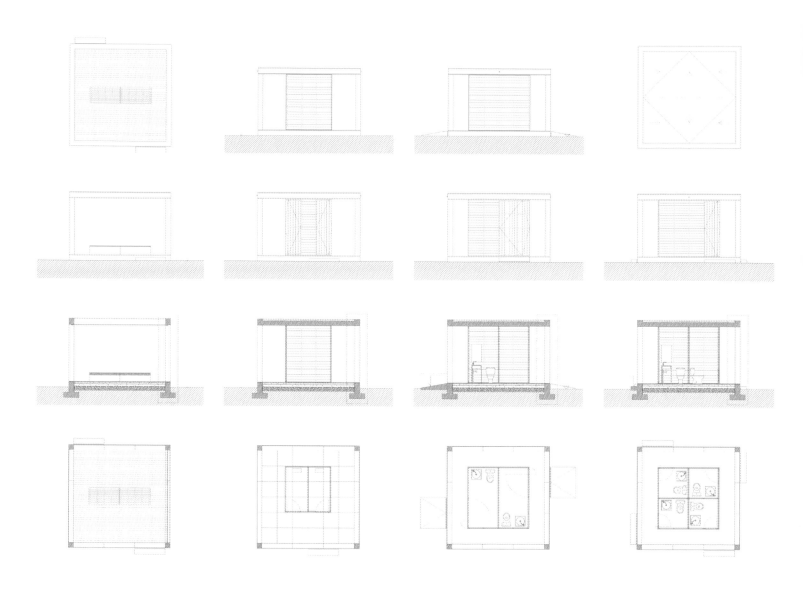

A series of modular pavilions (each containing a table and benches) are set throughout the park. Their placement has been based on the repetition of a simple element that unfolds to respond to different uses, sometimes made up of small groups, other times dispersed. Their placement is not random; quite the contrary, they are organized in an attempt to establish a punctuation in the territory.

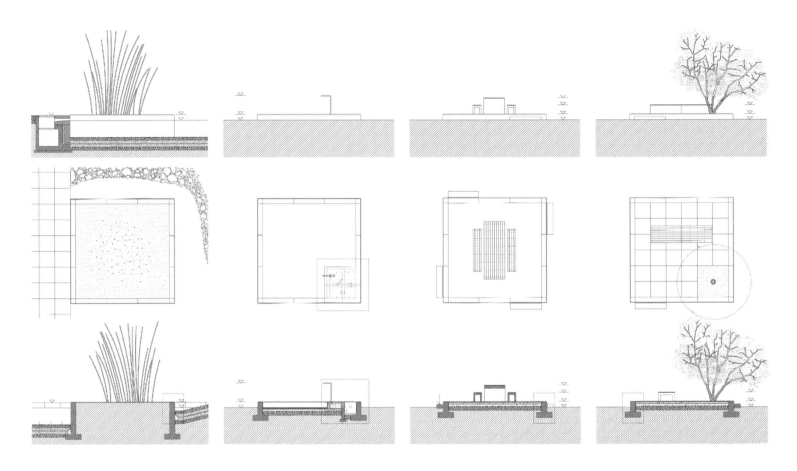

The physical boundaries shaping the plot are defined by the use of two distinctive materials, their respective construction techniques and consequent sensorial perception. They have been organized into two categories corresponding to the two realities that coexist in the territory: the urban context, with schools and a residential nucleus set adjacent to the street the park faces; and its rural character, constituted by a parcel of agricultural land.

Kovács, Lendvai, Muszbek, Pozsár, Tihanyi & Wallner
# Millenáris Park

Budapest, Hungary

2001 was a millennial year for Hungary, marking 1000 years since the founding of the state, which occurred in 1001, when St. Stephen was crowned. The biggest millenary investment of 2001 was the rehabilitation of the Ganz industrial area, on which a cultural center was placed with a reception and program hall, a theater and three exhibition buildings, all situated in the Millenium Park.

The park has been conceptually divided into two parts, one representing the idea of "motivation", the other standing for "creation" (in the interactive side of the park).

In the motivational part of the park visitors find themselves surrounded by the usual urban and natural environment, although, here, in an entirely unexpected form. Trees seem to grow out of the water of the lake; hills are bridged by a glass corridor that crosses a wheat field with shrubs forming cut bales. If you deprive these elements of their original environmental context and put them into a different surrounding, you are able to examine them freely and they become a source of inspiration.

Leaving the motivational area, one reaches the interactive space, the playground of creativity. Here visitors find all the environmental elements that they encountered on the way put into mobile form.

Overall, the park can be thought of as one large contiguous space. There are no formal elements creating borderlines that would break the continuity of the different spaces. The notion that defines the spaces in the park is not that of functionality, but rather a projection of the process of creating.

The park was opened to the public in July 2001. Attention has been drawn not only to the park itself, but also to the cultural events that are organized by a public benefit organization (Millenáris Kht.), which was established especially for this reason. Along with the indoor exhibitions, which take place all year round, in the summer and early autumn the park offers such outdoor events as statue exhibitions, fashion shows, classical music concerts, special programs for children and so on. As these events are free to the general public, this park differs from all others in Budapest, and revives the traditional aspects of the public parks built at the end of the 19th century.

**Photographs: Péter Hapák, Samu Szemerey**

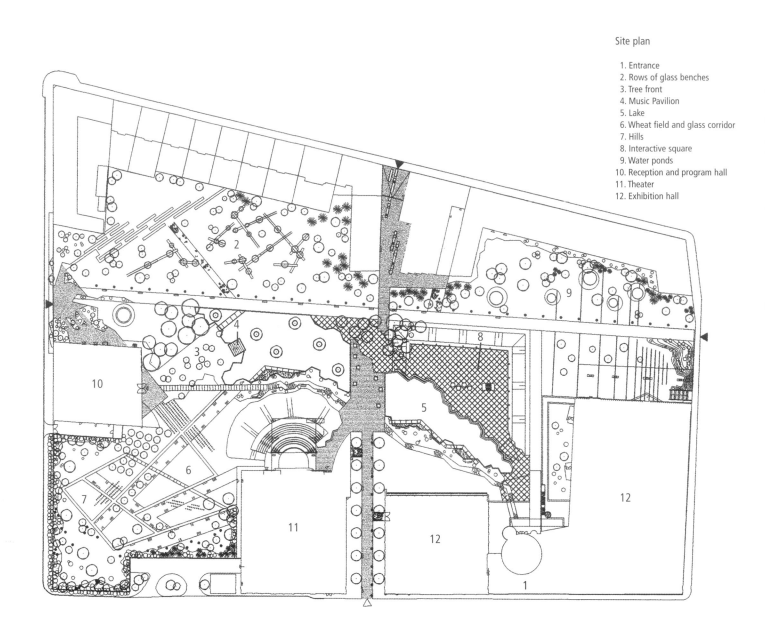

Site plan

1. Entrance
2. Rows of glass benches
3. Tree front
4. Music Pavilion
5. Lake
6. Wheat field and glass corridor
7. Hills
8. Interactive square
9. Water ponds
10. Reception and program hall
11. Theater
12. Exhibition hall

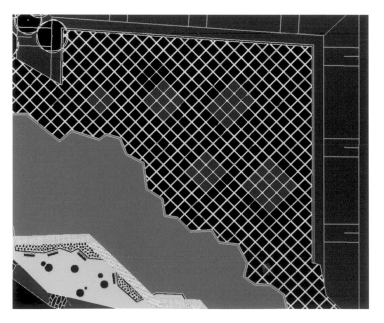

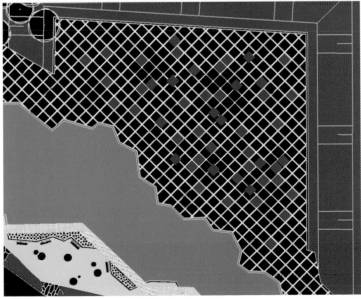

The establishment of the park played an important role in the fresh air supply of this part of the city (most fresh air previously came from the surrounding hills of Buda), since it lies at a point where the air channel is obstructed by a densely built district. The demolition of almost 70% of the former factory's relatively high buildings was the first step in the recovery of the air channel.

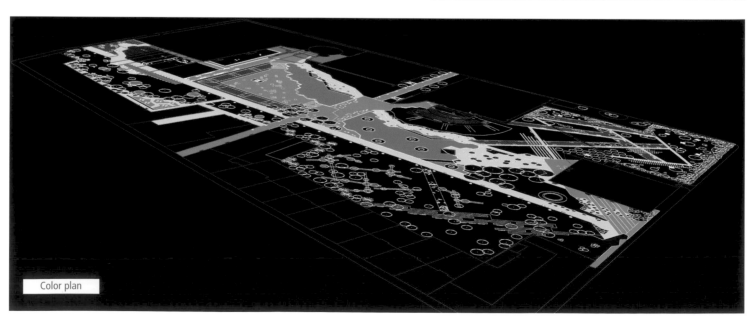

Color plan

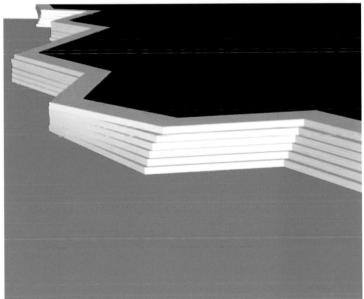

The oil-contaminated soil and groundwater were purified via a drainage system; percolating rainwater was collected in drainage pipes, which was extracted with the groundwater, while clean water was pumped in.

The conditions of the former industrial area's rehabilitation were: demolitions (the only buildings retained were those designated as industrial monuments), the exchange of soil (up to 1m of depth) and the managing of industrial waste and contamination.

[ Stig L. Andersson

# The Anchor Park

Malmö, Sweden

The layout of this park does not depend on formal principles, but rather is solely determined by matter and composition. It has been conceived as an injection of nature to counterbalance the predictable order of the surrounding town. The focus on vegetation (and its interaction with climate) has been proposed as atonement for human-made perfection.

The park's biotopes include seven strains of grass in a variety of types: some are fast growing, some tall and fragile, others very green and moist. Each of them, however, contributes to the creation of specific spatial qualities. Instead of being just surface coverings, they offer a scheme of overlapping systems of sequences and open progressions that highlight their individual textural variations and qualities.

At the same time, they all respond to the wind on a constant basis, just as the circular stamps on the concrete slab react to humidity. Whatever the weather, it can be seen on its physical interaction with the stamps; because the omnipresent water will be expressed differently whether in the form of ice, dryness, dust or moisture.

Neither the grass, nor any other material, requires the slightest maintenance from the park authorities; on the contrary, any sort of tampering would counteract the architect's intentions.

This is even more the case with the biotopes. The biotopes are four well-defined landscape types, the alder marsh, oak woods, willow woods and beech woods, each of which owes its existence to micro-organic processes. They stand in a divided meadow with seven different varieties of grass that are sharply separated as distinct mono-cultures, raised and bordered by steel edgings.

This area had been a defunct harbor area before being transformed into an urban district. Subsequently, the Anchor Park is an attempt to bring together a range of materials —concrete, tarmac, grass, wood and iron— in a contemporary reference to the past.

The result is a surprising and unforeseen interaction of materials, adding a new didactic dimension to the experience of people every time they visit the park. Only time will determine its final aspect.

**Photographs: Jens Linde/Sla, Åke E: Son Lindman, Torben Peterson**

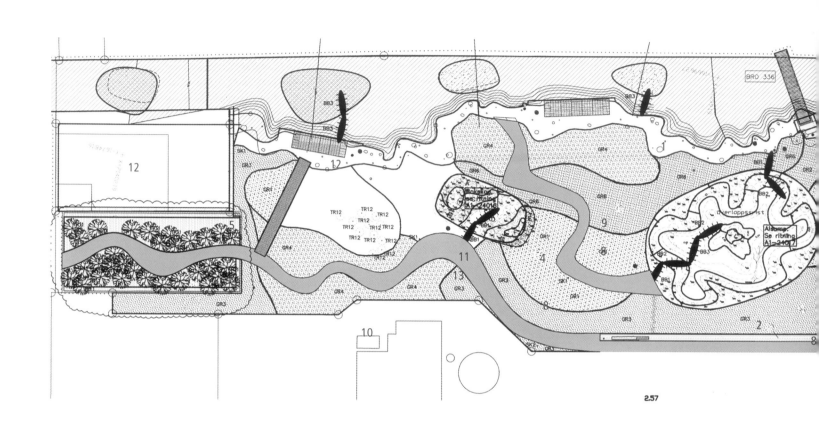

2.57

152

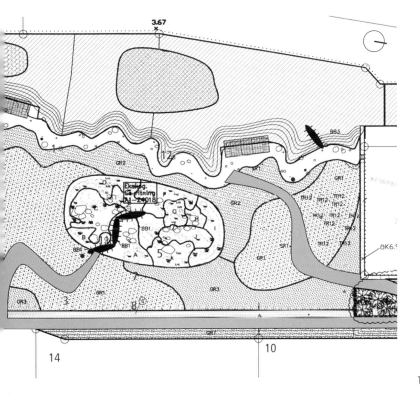

General floor plan

1. Water
2. Alder marsh
3. Oak
4. Forest
5. Beech forest
6. Stepping bugs
7. Meadow
8. Tentacles
9. Seafront
10. Pine
11. Resting site
12. Seaweed biotope
13. Wood bridges
14. Veranda

The park's biotopes are four well-defined landscape types: the alder marsh, oak woods, willow woods and beech woods, which owe their existence to micro-organic processes. They stand in a divided meadow with seven different varieties of grass, each raised and bordered by steel edgings; none of which requires the slightest maintenance from park authorities.

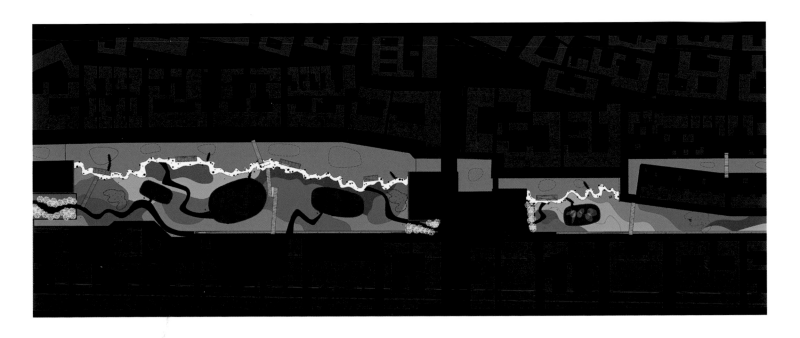

Fixture details

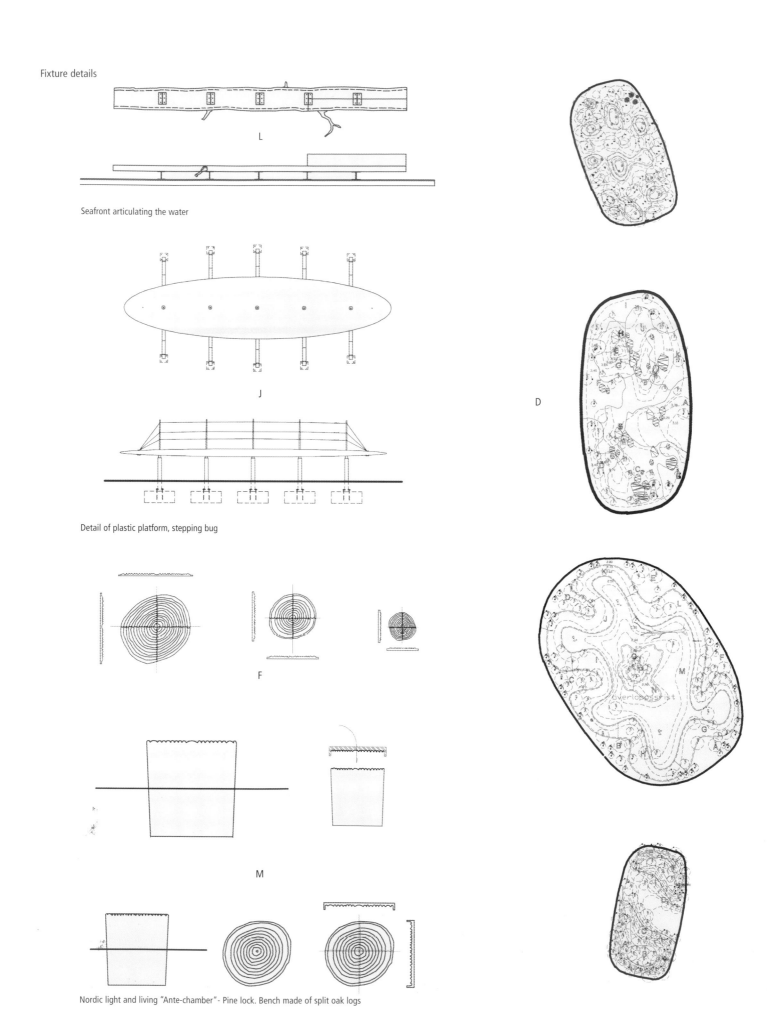

L

Seafront articulating the water

J

Detail of plastic platform, stepping bug

F

M

Nordic light and living "Ante-chamber" - Pine lock. Bench made of split oak logs

D

154

Tabula natura

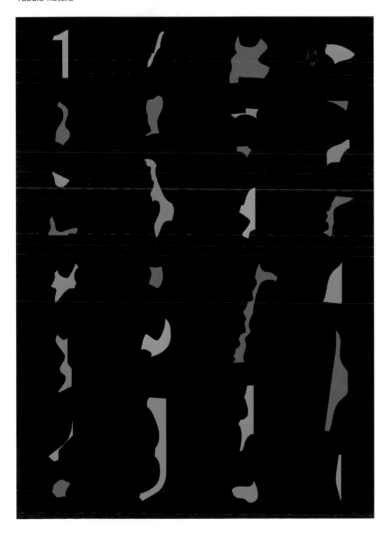

## Florence Mercier

# Le Grand Mail du Parc des Lilas

Vitry sur Seine, Val de Marne. France

As a first phase in the Parc des Lilas (occupying 100 hectares), the Grand Mail is located on an extensive cultivated plot of 1000x100 meters, facing westward toward the Family Gardens created by Latiere and Michel Leroy next to the new urban complexes of the city of Thiais and to the east of the Vitry pavilions.

The limits of this new garden are boldly defined, although it remains open to the exterior. With walking routes winding their way all throughout the park, it was particularly important to plan each section of the paths and to create a rhythm within the space. The resulting program is sculpted by memory-inducing images with their corresponding places.

A meticulous smoothing out of the differences in ground level has given new value to the breadth of the park, making use of the natural gently rising and falling terrain and offering an interplay of contrasts between the horizontal trunks of the oaks and the change in level at the banks of the Flower Canal.

Three basic elements make up the Grand Mail: a row of oaks and the Flower Canal; a large central lawn; and small groves of trees.

At the park's southern border Quercos Frainetto (a species of oak with leaves resembling those of an ash tree) are aligned in rows marking the main walking route.

A number of points of interest have been created in order to attract visitors toward the cedar and pine forest, where the views end.

The canal of flowers is located within an old quarry. The Mercier team used water as a poetic metaphor and planted pulses and perennials to evoke the movement of water. Rock-filled gabions were placed along the banks. Here, the large flower beds evoke the fluidity of the water: the pulses and lavender are the backdrop to the overall floral scene and their flowerings give the canal a different look during each season. Bridges span the canal at regular intervals, providing a certain rhythm to the path and creating different vantage points.

One of the parks most extensive areas is the tree-lined meadow, around which are scattered a number of spaces intended for both private and public use – spaces such as horticultural gardens, nurseries, rose beds, and family gardens.

The northern lawn, which provides wide open recreational spaces, is accessed from the main tree-lined walkway via a series of bridges spanning the canal. There are also small patches of fruit trees conforming to the natural original curves of the terrain.

Different species and sizes of trees intermingle in rows at the northern end, sculpting spaces between them.

Finally, groves of pine and cedar crown the far western portion of the Grand Mail.

Owner: Conseil Général Val de Marne

Parc des Lilas programming: J. Varier-Gandois

Grand mail: Florence Mercier, landscaper

**Photographs: Florence Mercier, Hervé Abbadie**

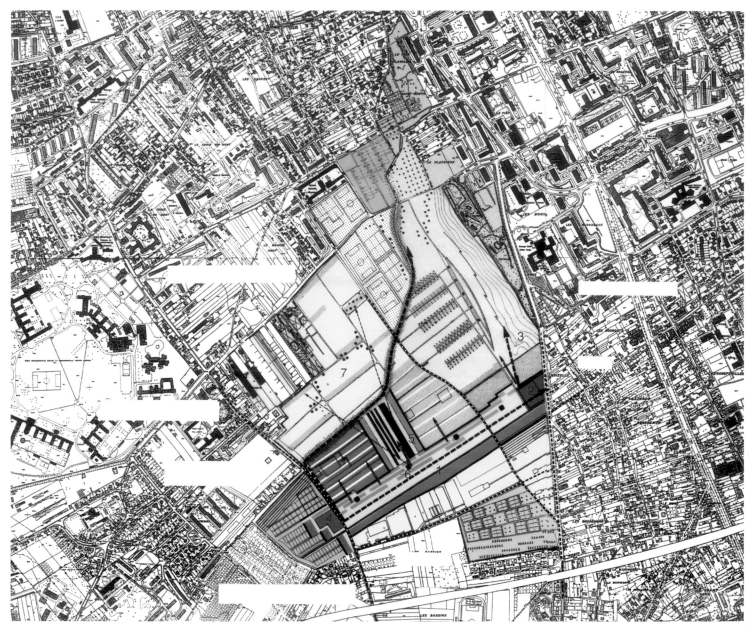

**Site plan**. Relation between Grand Mail and the Parc des Lilas

| | |
|---|---|
| Open space | → Access |
| Family gardens | ▪ Differential sequence |
| Rose beds | --- Border |
| Tree-lined leg of footpath | → Range of views |
| Nursery | |
| Horticulture | 1 Mail: Independent entity related to |
| Cultural center of city | its surroundings |
| Area for sports | 2 Access |
| Parking | 3 Relation to batters |
| Mail | 4 End of Mail: Point of attention and |
| Canals (with water or plants) | transition to the family gardens |
| Shrubbery | |
| Point of interest (specific program) | 5 Fountain |
| ━━ Footpath | 6 Vantage point |
| •••• Vehicular access | 7 Landscape design and field recom- |
| | position |

As a first phase in the Parc des Lilas (occupying 100 hectares), the Grand Mail is located on an extensive cultivated plot of 1000x100 meters, facing westward toward the Family Gardens created by Latiere and Michel Leroy next to the new urban complexes of the city of Thiais and to the east of the Vitry pavilions.

Longitudinal section

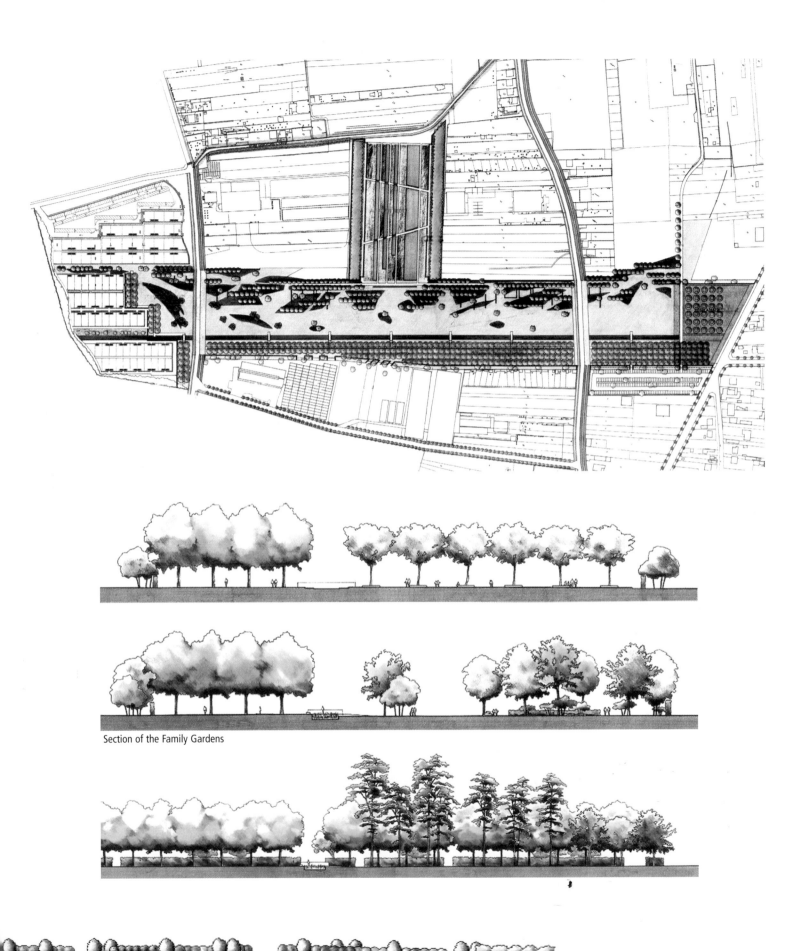

Section of the Family Gardens

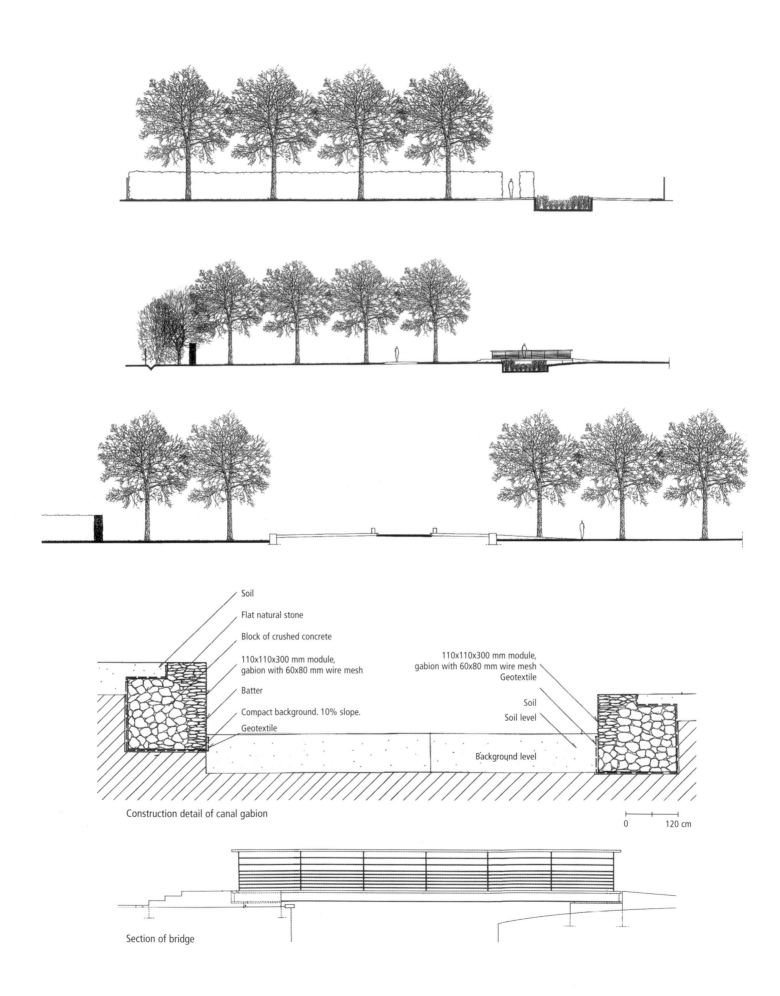

Soil

Flat natural stone

Block of crushed concrete

110x110x300 mm module,
gabion with 60x80 mm wire mesh

Batter

Compact background. 10% slope.

Geotextile

110x110x300 mm module,
gabion with 60x80 mm wire mesh

Geotextile

Soil

Soil level

Background level

Construction detail of canal gabion

0          120 cm

Section of bridge

Located in an old quarry where it was impossible to extract water, the Flower Canal is an attractive and poetic space. Mercier's plan used the metaphor of water for the creation of this canal, which has been planted with pulses and perennials, evoking the movement of water. The banks are lined with rock-filled gabions. The bridges, which span the canal at regular intervals, provide a sense of rhythm and create different vantage points.

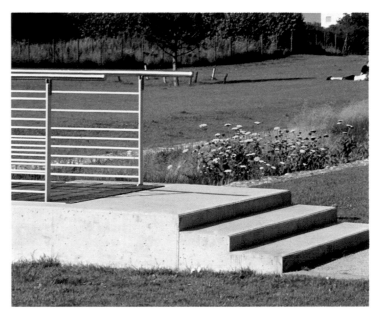

Group composition of wild plants in the Flower Canal

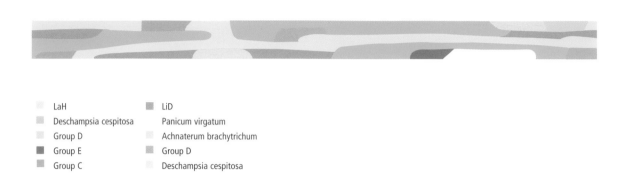

| | |
|---|---|
| ▢ LaH | ▢ LiD |
| ▢ Deschampsia cespitosa | Panicum virgatum |
| ▢ Group D | ▢ Achnaterum brachytrichum |
| ▉ Group E | ▢ Group D |
| ▢ Group C | ▢ Deschampsia cespitosa |

Group A

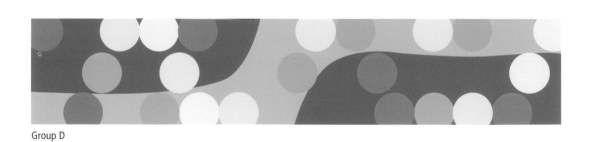

Group D

| | |
|---|---|
| ▉ Lychnis flor-cuculi (11 units) | Hemerocallis "Aten" (6 units) |
| ▢ Veronica longifolia "Exalta" (7 units) | ▢ Iris germanica "Invitation" (6 units) |
| ▢ Lychnis flor-cuculi (7 units) | ▢ Iris germanica "Jane Philip" (6 units) |
| ▢ Echinops ritro "Veitch'2 blue" (4 units) | ▉ Iris germanica "Son of Star" ( 6 units) |

The row of oaks is one of Grand Mail's central elements. At the park's southern border Quercos Frainetto (a species of oak with leaves resembling those of an ash tree) are aligned in rows marking the main walking route.

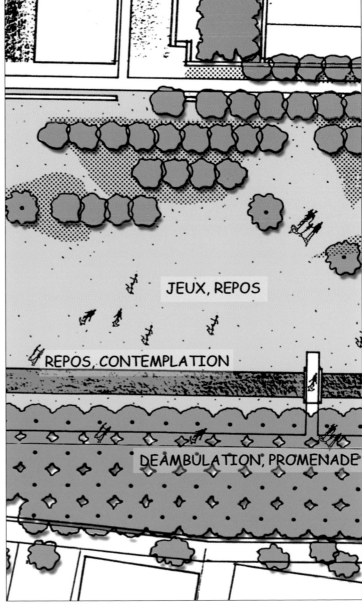

## Ramón Pico + Javier López
## Sendero del Pinar de la Algaida

El Puerto de Santa María, Spain

The greatest virtue of this project was present in its very inception: with the proposed footpath, the city would reclaim a derelict and forgotten area, the previously inaccessible outlying fringes consisting of a defunct salt works and a neighboring pine grove.

The completely flat and horizontal nature of the mudflats was a highly inviting aspect. This interminable horizontal surface was made up of mud plains and tidelands, all of which was interspersed by salt flats, which were in some places superimposed onto the visually interesting textural contrasts of water, soil and plant life. In the background, as a natural counterpoint, is a pine grove.

Three separate, yet interwoven, ecosystems share this site: La Salina de los Desamparados, an area of swamplands enclosed by dykes; the virgin mudflats, a natural landscape made up of stretches of swamp vegetation cleaved by winding tidelands and a drainage system; and the pine grove, which was mostly left in its original state.

The idea behind the footpath was that it should bring the three recognized units together so that they could be turned into a suitable spot for taking a break or getting together with friends. At the same time, it should recuperate what were once the natural wonders of the site. The route decided upon for the footpath was chosen with all of this in mind. Like a thread pulling the disparate elements of the landscape together, it roams at will over the areas which have already been artificially broken up, areas such as the wall lying on the outskirts of the salt flats and the existing footpaths in the pine grove.

The materials used follow sustainability criteria, with the recycled products of grinding the waste material from the neighboring towns forming the foundation and finishes. Wherever the path does not meet an existing structure, it becomes a raised platform, which enables unobstructed circulation beneath the canals and marshes.

Nonetheless, the beneficent and recuperative stance that characterized the program involved a great deal of risk: that of tempering the site excessively, allowing the restoration of environmental purity to erase the imprints of the past.

The project had to maintain something of that ruggedness and ambiguity which we find today in these mudflats. Thus, the places chosen for contemplation of the landscape were given a certain "leftover" feel, like remains left by a receding tide: a jumble of wood or a large fold of half-buried scrap metal that provides shelter for passersby.

**Photographs: Fernando Alda**

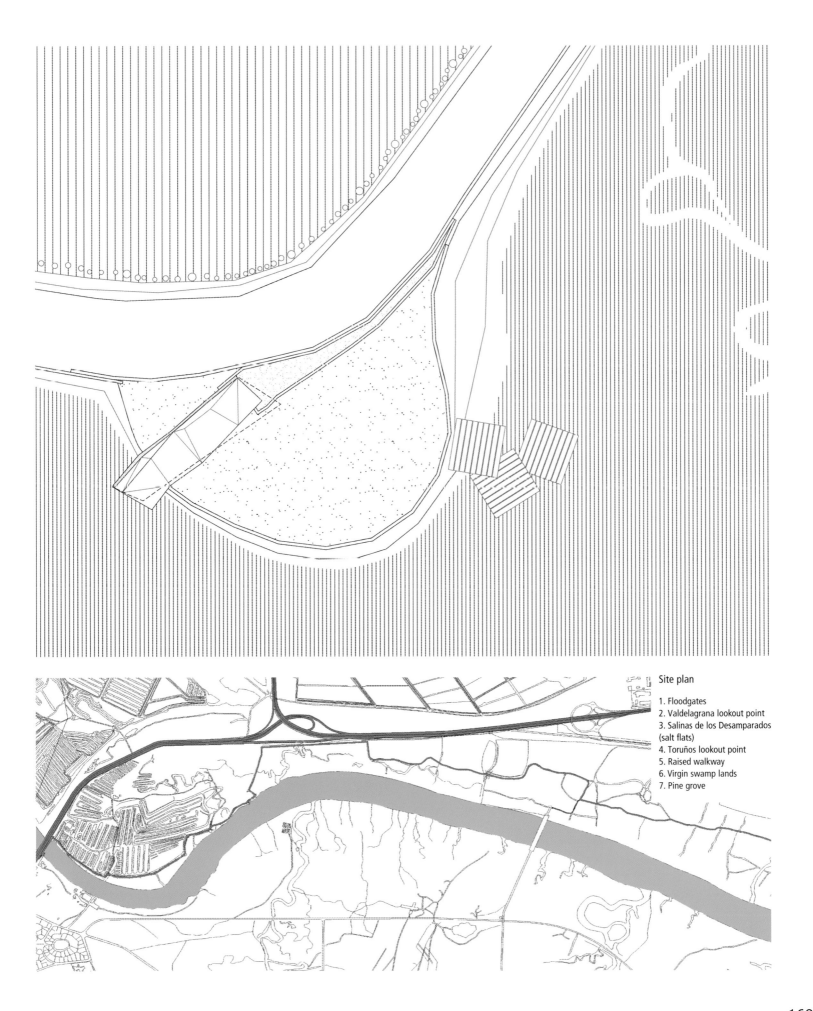

Site plan

1. Floodgates
2. Valdelagrana lookout point
3. Salinas de los Desamparados (salt flats)
4. Toruños lookout point
5. Raised walkway
6. Virgin swamp lands
7. Pine grove

The materials used follow sustainability criteria, with the recycled products of grinding the waste material from the neighboring towns forming the foundation and finishes. Wherever the path does not meet an existing structure, it becomes a raised platform, which enables unobstructed circulation beneath the canals and marshes.

The places chosen for stopping and resting, for contemplation of the landscape, were given a certain "leftover" feel, like the remains left behind by a receding tide: a jumble of wood or a large fold of half-buried scrap metal that provides shelter for passersby.

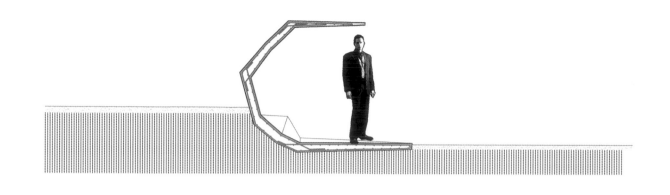

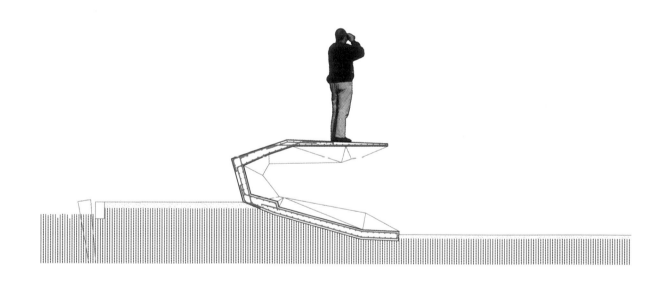

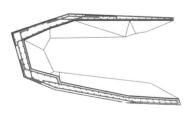